PENGUIN BOOKS

Gangs

Born in Essex in 1964, Ross Kemp is best known for his portrayal of
Grant Mitchell in *EastEnders*. His father was a senior detective with the
Metropolitan Police force, and as a result crime has always fascinated
Kemp.

Ross Kemp on Gangs is an award-winning series on Sky One.

Gangs

ROSS KEMP

PENGUIN BOOKS

PENGUIN BOOKS

Published by the Penguin Group
Penguin Books Ltd, 80 Strand, London WC2R ORL, England
Penguin Group (USA) Inc., 375 Hudson Street, New York, New York 10014, USA
Penguin Group (Canada), 90 Eglinton Avenue East, Suite 700, Toronto, Ontario, Canada M4P 2Y3
(a division of Pearson Penguin Canada Inc.)
Penguin Ireland, 25 St Stephen's Green, Dublin 2, Ireland
(a division of Penguin Books Ltd)
Penguin Group (Australia), 250 Camberwell Road, Camberwell, Victoria 3124, Australia
(a division of Pearson Australia Group Pty Ltd)
Penguin Books India Pvt Ltd, 11 Community Centre, Panchsheel Park, New Delhi – 110 017, India
Penguin Group (NZ), 67 Apollo Drive, Rosedale, North Shore 0632, New Zealand
(a division of Pearson New Zealand Ltd)
Penguin Books (South Africa) (Pty) Ltd, 24 Sturdee Avenue,
Rosebank, Johannesburg 2196, South Africa

Penguin Books Ltd, Registered Offices: 80 Strand, London WC2R ORL, England

www.penguin.com

First published by Michael Joseph 2007
Published in Penguin Books 2008

6

Copyright © Ross Kemp, 2007

Photography courtesy of Ross Kemp and British Sky Broadcasting Limited

Set in 13/15.75 pt Monotype Garamond
Typeset by Rowland Phototypesetting Ltd, Bury St Edmunds, Suffolk
Printed in England by Clays Ltd, St Ives plc

ISBN: 978-0-141-03225-2

www.greenpenguin.co.uk

Mixed Sources
Product group from well-managed
forests and other controlled sources
www.fsc.org Cert no. SA-COC-1592
© 1996 Forest Stewardship Council

Penguin Books is committed to a sustainable future
for our business, our readers and our planet.
The book in your hands is made from paper
certified by the Forest Stewardship Council.

Contents

Introduction

The AK-47 was fully loaded, safety catch off and was so close to my face that I could taste the metal. The fact that this weapon was in the control of a teenager who was 'off his face' on coke was clearly of some concern to me. But the really frightening part was looking into his vacant eyes as he fingered the trigger – in his world the price of life is worthless. It is at moments like this that I often wonder how I have got myself and the crew into this kind of situation. That's when I have to remind myself that it was my idea to be there in the first place! And if we didn't take control of the situation very quickly my epitaph would be, 'Bloody idiot!'

Three years earlier I was standing on an LA sidewalk talking to a gangster who had been shot more than two dozen times (as you do) when the questions came to me: 'Why hasn't anyone made a television series about gangs?', 'Why do people join them?', 'What makes a gangster tick?' and 'Why do they do what they do and how do they do it?' I wondered if gang membership was really on the increase and, if so, why was it happening? With gang violence a growing problem in my own city, London, I wanted to find out.

Like many things in life, the *Gangs* series came about by accident. In 2005, Sky Television asked me to step in as a presenter on *Lethal Attraction*, a programme about America's deadly love affair with firearms. While filming in Compton, a gang-infested suburb of Los Angeles, I met a leader of the Bloods gang called Hound Dog. Little did I know this was to have a profound effect on the next five years of my life.

Hound Dog operated in the Rolling Twenties, between 21st Street and 29th Street, where a lot of gang action goes down. We're talking war – a war of attrition for turf, supremacy, money and kudos waged on a daily basis between the two main gangs, the Bloods and the Crips. A war that started in 1969 and has been going on ever since.

Well built and physically fit, Hound Dog had a small teardrop tattooed under his right eye, dreadlocks with red plastic bobbles on the ends of the plaits and an easy-going, open manner. He was highly intelligent and charismatic. He talked about life and death in a plain, matter of fact way. He was engaging and articulate, and we both knew that if fortune had dealt him different cards and he had been born two miles up the road he might have gone to college. As it was, Hound Dog lived in a Bloods enclave totally surrounded by Crips. This wasn't a healthy location. In fact it was so toxic he told me he had been shot twenty-seven times. At first I didn't believe him. How could any human being take that many bullets and survive? It had to be some

2

kind of world record. Either that or a miracle. Seeing my reaction he said, 'You don't believe me? Most people don't believe me.' He pulled up his shirt, lowered his jeans and counted off the wounds one by one. It was true: his body was starred, notched and riveted with entry and exit wounds. The man was a walking testament to modern medical science – and the most incredible luck. He said, 'Put your fingers in these, man,' trying to get me to feel the depth of his wounds.

Hound Dog had spent so much time in ER he knew more about anatomy – especially his own – than most medical students. He'd taken nine rounds in the chest and three to the ribs. He knew exactly how to treat a wound, what type of bullet inflicted what damage, and how likely the body was to survive a certain gunshot in a given spot. As he lay unconscious on the ground in the course of one shooting, one of his attackers had run up, put the muzzle of a 9-millimetre pistol up under his chin and pulled the trigger. It was meant to make sure he died. Instead, the round went up into his mouth, blew off the tip of his tongue, ripped out the left side of his nose, re-entered at the top of the left eye socket, skimmed across his forehead and then stuck fast. It had to be cut out. He lifted up the red and white 'rag' – Bloods bandanna – he wore to show me the neat scar where the bullet had been removed. By any spin of the dice Hound Dog should have been dead. Instead, he'd had his chest split and cranked wide and his spleen removed along with lots of lead.

The shooting had begun as soon as he joined the gang. The young Hound Dog had been leaning in through a window selling marijuana. 'What will you take?' he had asked his customers. 'Your life,' they said, and shot him six times in the groin as he reared back. One bullet hit a testicle. 'Hey, but look,' Hound Dog told me with a grin. 'It's all right – I still got two kids!'

Hound Dog was a scary guy. But scary or not, fully fledged Bloods gang member Hound Dog lived in a 24/7 world of fear. He didn't have a nice house in Beverly Hills; he had a very small house in one of the worst parts of south LA with a blocked toilet and small, airless rooms. He didn't have an open-top Mercedes or loads of bling, and he didn't have a pneumatic young blonde hanging round the place in designer lingerie. He had a large wife with a baby on each hip, and every time a car slowed down outside he reached for the MAC-10 sub-machine gun he kept ready or one of his many other automatic weapons, or the .38 Smith & Wesson revolver he had in case the automatic weapons jammed. Standing in the front room of his house he said, 'If a car slows down, you gotta get down 'cos I'm gonna start shooting.'

Hound Dog kept a lot of domestic bleach in the house to remove his DNA from the firearms after use. He knew how to strip and clean his arsenal blindfold. I've worked with the British army a bit and it was like talking to a soldier – in his case, a south LA street soldier. Violence was his stock-in-trade. He lived on the front line of a routine relentless war.

In case you think I am exaggerating, while we were filming, one of Hound Dog's buddies, TK, got shot in the back by two rival gang members. He couldn't afford medical care, so the hospital did what it could and then asked him to leave. Another gang member, Rat, let TK stay at his parents' place, but after one night they grew understandably nervous and asked their badly wounded house guest to leave. When I interviewed TK we both knew he was dying. Forty-eight hours later he died alone on the street.

Not a good way to live or die. Nothing glorious about it.

We had to leave in a rush when it looked as if there might be shooting – apparently the local Crips were jealous of the attention. Back in my hotel room, I tried emptying the minibar to calm my nerves. Sitting on the edge of the bed, I thought it over. There must be lots of Hound Dogs out there with stories to tell – stories that were fascinating but which, if Hound Dog and his mates were anything to go by, demolished the myth you see in movies and music videos, the myth that gangs are sexy, glamorous and cool. The idea that firearms are somehow fun and using them makes you a big man. Was the 'gangsta cool' image we see so much of just so much hype? What about a series that lifted the stone and set out to find the truth? I called Jackie Lawrence, then a factual programmes commissioning editor at Sky Television: 'If I can find more people like Hound Dog out there on the streets, there's a series to be made.' Without a moment's hesitation, Jackie gave me the green light.

My brother Darren is an award-winning documentary filmmaker and my wife is a journalist. I have many reporter friends in the field, but I am not a journalist. I'm an actor, and I don't go at stories in the same way. Actors are generally interested in the way people behave. I don't have an agenda, an angle, or anything like that.

My father was in the Metropolitan Police. When he was a Detective Inspector and I was around nine years old, I opened his briefcase, something I was forbidden to do. Inside I found a set of crime photographs showing the dead body of a white male dumped in scrubland. The sun had cooked parts of his skin black. The police initially thought the victim had been run over. It turned out that the killers had kicked and stamped on his chest so hard they had collapsed his ribcage. The corpse was drilled and mined by maggots.

I felt sick at what I saw but, at the same time, fascinated. My dad came home, found out what I had done, and I got the biggest telling off I've ever had. Then he sat down and explained to me what had happened to the victim. I was intrigued. With tours on the Sweeney (Flying Squad) and with the Regional Crime Squad he spent a lot of time around human suffering and violence. This is one of the very rare occasions he talked about his work and it was rarely discussed again. But, like my father, I am interested in finding out about what motivates people to cause each other harm.

There have been countless times over the last five years when I have longed to be back in the safe fictional world of Albert Square or the battles of *Ultimate Force* in the comfort of Pinewood Studios. I've spent considerable time in some of the worst prisons on the planet and countless hours with murderers, rapists and assassins. At times, undoubtedly, I have been deeply affected by what I have witnessed. At others, I have found myself sharing a beer and a joke with a multiple murderer. I would say now that this book leaves more questions than answers. Gangs are not a new phenomenon, however, their membership is on the increase globally.

I have been privileged to travel the world over the years and discover countries and cultures that I wasn't aware existed. I hope by reading this book you too will be able to gain an insight into some of the most dangerous and, I think, most interesting people on the planet.

1. Rio de Janeiro

Rio de Janeiro is a city at war with itself – it's just that no one has declared it openly yet. When we got to the airport on the first leg of my journey to investigate some of the world's most dangerous gangs, Ivan, one of the city's hardbitten taxi drivers, drove me in through the northern suburbs to my hotel on Copacabana Beach. The potholed four-lane motorway snaked in past a motley collection of half-finished offices and grimy apartment blocks, functioning and abandoned factories, warehouses and parking lots, and there, glowering from the steep, loaf-shaped hillsides that rose all around us, were Rio's 800-plus favelas, or shanty towns.

Up there was where the gangs lived. Up there was where I needed to go.

Like avalanches of crime and resentment waiting to sweep down and engulf the city, Rio's favelas are home to some of the world's poorest people and some of its most violent gangs. With worrying frequency, the gangsters do come to town – mugging, looting, burning and killing.

As we bowled past long stretches that looked as if someone had forgotten to finish them, Ivan asked what I was doing in Rio. When I explained I was there to do a programme for Sky Television on the city's gangs, he burst out laughing. 'What's so funny?' I asked.

He gestured at the rubbish-strewn ground either side of the shimmering asphalt. 'See this *autoroute* we are on? We call it the Gaza Strip. On one side you got the Comando Vermelho gang. CV are the strongest gang in Rio; they run most of the favelas. On the other side, you got the Amigos dos Amigos – the Friends of Friends. When night comes, the gangs start shooting at each other – sometimes even during the day. You don't want to drive down here after dark, my friend, or you get your head blown off.'

Before we got any further, we hit a police roadblock. This wasn't anything like a UK police checkpoint – sinister in black, these policemen bristled with weapons: M16s, shotguns and semi-automatic pistols. Seeing a gringo in the back of the cab, they waved us through; as far as they were concerned, I was just another tourist on my way to the fleshpots. 'What are they looking for?' I asked Ivan.

'Gang members,' he said and drove through the barrier. 'Drugs. Money. Kidnap victims. Stolen goods. You name it.' Swerving to avoid a pothole, Ivan took a hand off the steering wheel and gestured lazily. 'Look at the walls.' I looked, wondering if he was trying to wind me up. He wasn't – most of the high concrete walls, peeling paint, were pockmarked with bullet strikes. Sometimes you could see quite plainly the work of heavy-calibre weapons.

'OK, mate,' I said. 'That's very reassuring.'

As we drove on, Ivan told me there are many of these Gaza Strips in Rio de Janeiro, front lines between the city's warring gangs locked in a deadly struggle for control of the drugs trade. Another of the crossfire cross-routes is known locally as the Lebanon. The fighting that goes on around it is as bad as the bloody civil strife that ravaged Beirut in the 1980s.

As we turned onto the six-lane motorway that separates Rio de Janeiro's long curving beachfronts from the city behind, the whole picture changed: this was the Rio of the guidebooks, the downtown area fronting some of the world's most famous beaches – Ipanema, Copacabana and Leblon – backed by soaring hotels, tall, swaggering apartment blocks and what looked like glitzy shopping malls. At face value, it was easy to see how Rio had come by its reputation as one of the world's sexiest and most glamorous cities. Set in a spectacular curving bay, the city enjoys one of the world's most wonderful locations. There was the soaring Sugar Loaf Mountain in the distance; the scenery and the weather were beautiful; and even though the sun had dropped below the horizon, there were lots of not bad-looking people wearing not very much clothing.

Checking into our hotel, I was greeted with the news that Jason Evans, our assistant producer for the shoot, had already been mugged by four kids. I was beginning to think leaving my Rolex Submariner watch at home might have been a smart move. Peter Wery, our Brazilian cameraman, had lived in the Netherlands for many years and was ex-Dutch special forces. Cool in a tight spot, he had been in a few of them. Jason had been preparing the ground. He was already on very good terms with the local street robbers, but clearly not all of them. There was also Tim Pritchard, the director, who specializes in South American stories and handily speaks Brazilian Portuguese.

We had found ourselves some local fixers, who would hopefully know how to handle the gangs. Born and brought up in Rio, Fernando Continentino, our short, smiling, blue-eyed local translator/fixer who always had a Marlboro Red on the go, was one of my main contact points with the gangs. Our soundman, Heron de Alencar, was also Brazilian – very bright and never stuck for a word. He got by on charm when all else failed. I made a mental note to be respectful: whatever I might find here, Fernando and Heron probably wouldn't appreciate my coming down too hard on the city.

Once installed in the hotel, we went out to find some dinner. It was late by now, but the beachfront was buzzing. No one looked as if the idea of sleeping troubled them much, and judging by the street urchins racing around in little packs – the kind Jason had warned us about – when they did sleep they kept one eye open to make sure no one ripped them off. The more time I spent wandering around, the less I felt Rio lived up to its glamorous reputation. It looks good from a distance, but even one block back from the glittering strip it goes rapidly downhill. There are bright flashing lights everywhere you look, more fast-food joints than you can shake a stick at and lots of very young girls walking arm in arm with equal numbers of very old American tourists. Shops sell fake designer clothing and tawdry souvenirs; dodgy saunas advertise rent boys. In fact, if I had closed one eye and ignored the Americans I could have been in Soho in London, only it was a whole lot hotter and the women were wearing even less.

But the place was extremely alive – everyone animated, everyone busy. Even getting on for midnight, there were kids queuing on the beach to play keepy-uppy football on the volleyball courts – you have to stop the ball touching the ground, using only your feet and head. No wonder the Brazilians are so good at the 'beautiful game'. The world's most flamboyant carnival wasn't actually on when we were there, but with the thumping music, the racket from the street and the general level of hustle and bustle it felt as if one was about to start up at any moment.

I tried out my Spanglish on the waiter. He ignored me – not to be rude, but because as a speaker of the harsh, Hungarian-sounding Rio Portuguese, he didn't understand a word of what I was saying. Following my gaze, which had settled on a group of stick-thin local girls hovering in the restaurant entrance, Heron said,

'The girls are thin like that because they are hungry, not because they are on a diet.' The more I looked around the more I noticed hungry people.

Next morning, bright and early, a man from the insurance company handed each of us a set of body armour before we went off to try to talk to some gangs. Fernando's upper lip curled. 'If you go into a favela wearing that stuff, the gangsters will shoot you just to see if it works.' You never saw three people strip off anything so quickly. But I felt less safe without it. I'm not ashamed to admit I was really worried about going into the first favela Fernando had arranged for us to visit, the Morro do Borel.

With one of the highest crime rates in South America, Brazil's favelas have a fearsome and well-deserved reputation for violence and death. In a conurbation of some six million people, Rio witnessed 6,620 murders in 2004, 6,438 in 2005, and 5,232 in the first ten months of 2006. A total of 18,290 killings in less than three years, the vast majority of them shootings, this was about six times the number of US troops killed in Iraq over the same period. The figures for São Paulo are even worse.

As we moved uphill towards the favela, things rapidly started turning worse. The approach route looked, smelt and felt like the entrance to an underworld. This is gang country, where outsiders tread at extreme risk. My guide to the Borel gang was MC Catra, a tall, laid-back former CV gang member turned master of ceremonies or rap artist. Catra is a favela celebrity who specializes in a style of music called *baile funk* – funk dance. Four-square and personable in his cut-off T-shirt, Catra made it plain he was a bit of a lad when it came to favela women. And as if to bear this out, they kept coming up to talk to him. On the morning we met, Catra was smoking a big, fat spliff. Judging by the slightly glassy look in his eyes it wasn't his first of the day. When he got to the end of one joint, Catra lit a new one from the roach. As a result, he got more and more stoned as the day wore on. Despite his default sullen expression and slightly menacing manner, Catra turned out to be chilled once he decided I had an open mind about the gangs, the favelas, and the people who lived in them, and was not looking to try anyone by television.

Adopted by a wealthy middle-class family as a small child, Catra was well educated – his English was a whole sight better than my Portuguese. Sadly for him, his adoptive parents split when he was sixteen, and the local authorities sent him back to live in the Borel shanties. Right away he fell in with the controlling Comando Vermelho gang, dealing drugs until his talent for music gave him a way out. That his brother still allegedly controlled part of the Borel drugs trade probably helped him get out of the gang alive, instead of leaving CV the usual way – feet first.

Like all Rio favelas, Catra explained, Borel is a drug-fuelled society that operates alongside and in direct opposition to local and national government. With a teeming population of about 25,000 – no one in officialdom has ever dared try to carry out a census – Borel squats on a broad, steep-backed hill to the north of the downtown area. Run by the CV gang, it is a bit like a medieval European city state. Distorted mirror images of the heavily guarded fortress compounds where Rio's rich live, favelas like Borel are gated communities, only instead of locking crime out, the favelas and the gangs that control them lock crime in.

There is only one road into and out of Borel. The checkpoint at the entrance is known as the *boca do fumo* – mouth of the smoke. There we found about two dozen heavily armed CV gang members on duty, ready to repel any attack by a rival gang or discourage one of the sporadic police raids. Foot soldiers, these gate guards are usually on a flat wage of around a thousand dollars a month, ten times the income of an average Rio labourer. With spotters and lookouts all around, the *boca do fumo* is the eyes and ears of the favela. The gangsters had a mixture of weaponry: FAL self-loading rifles, M16s, AK-47s and hand grenades. They also all had semi-automatic pistols holstered in proper, military-style webbing belts. The other meaning of *boca do fumo* is drugs outlet. Retail points for dealers and the users who come in to buy their drugs, mostly cocaine, the *bocas* are where the gangs make most of their money, and as such are vital parts of any favela.

Warned before going that filming at any of the *bocas*

would result in instant death by shooting, Peter kept the camera off and pointing at the ground. Looking at the expressions on the faces of our local crew, I took a mental pace back. They looked worried. Since I always take my cue as to how scared to be from the guys with local knowledge, that worried me.

After checking to make sure we were not armed or in league with the Rio police, the guards let us into Borel. As soon as I stepped inside the favela, waves of colour, sound and smell stopped me dead in my tracks. Everything was in sensory overdrive. Most of the shacks are made of a bright pink brick, many painted in garish colours and then daubed with graphic, violent murals and gang graffiti. In this favela, in a kind of gangster corporate branding, the lurid, scarlet scrawls of Comando Vermelho were everywhere. Small children dressed in football shirts and shorts darted about kicking plastic footballs, shouting and screaming and bumping into us; horns blaring, taxi bikes roared up and down the narrow, twisting streets and alleyways missing the throngs of brightly dressed people by a whisker; loud music blasted in the background and televisions roared out a mid-morning TV soap. A kaleidoscope of hand-painted shop signs advertised shoestring enterprises selling everything from stolen goods to bottled liquid petroleum gas and booze – especially booze and especially the favela favourite – big bottles of ice-cold Skol lager, chugged down fast before the intense heat has a chance to catch up with it.

An intoxicating mixture of marijuana smoke, barbecued meat, baked earth, garbage, sewage, petrol and diesel fumes and sweating humanity, the favela smelled like nowhere else I had been. I felt intensely alive in there, more than I ever had anywhere else. Everything was heightened; life was on fast forward; everyone looked happy, shouting and laughing and doing their deals. But at the same time I detected a strong undercurrent of tension, a sense that all of this could turn in a moment and not to the good.

Passionately loyal to Borel like almost all of its inhabitants, Catra had a colourful way with words when it came to describing his home. 'It feels, it laughs, it cries, it gets scared, it becomes tense,' he said, pausing only for a fresh puff of his spliff. Listening to the pulsating noise all around us, and watching the ebb and flow of some of the world's poorest, most disadvantaged and at the same time most interesting-looking people, I could see what he meant.

Built with maze-like, poorly lit alleyways and narrow streets on a steep slope that rises up through a broad gully from the skyscraper blocks of the city below and then gets steeper and steeper until you wonder how the jerry-built stilt houses cling to the cliff, Borel is a mudslide waiting to happen. The miracle is how some of the shacks remain upright and in one piece for as long as they do, given that they defy every principle and practice of sound building. From time to time, they don't: lacking proper foundations, if it rains these boxes can and do collapse down the hillsides like packs of cards. The poor-quality bricks don't help. So crumbly you can scratch a groove in them with a fingernail, they are also useless when it comes to stopping high-velocity bullets. During gunfights between gangs or between gang members and the police – and these are more or less a nightly occurrence – rounds tend to blast through your living-room wall and out the other side; it pays to throw yourself flat when the shooting starts. Having said which, some of the streets around me were paved, the construction work, Catra told me, paid for by CV – hearts and minds exercises designed to keep the people onside. Gangs will sometimes also put in street lighting or run water pipes or basic drainage. A few favelas like the city's biggest one, Rocinha, are showing signs of developing some real and lasting infrastructure. One day, if they continue to spruce themselves up and the gangs lose control, they may become part of the city instead of its bad neighbours.

In Rio, I realized, looking back across the city below, the poor hold the high ground while the rich live in the troughs between – the opposite of what happens just about everywhere else in the world. But then the rich know better – the hills might be cooler, but when the rains come the ground beneath the favelas can turn to slippery mud.

As the streets are mostly too narrow and twisting for cars, the two main ways of getting around favelas are on foot or by small motorbike or scooter. Driven at breakneck speed up and down the hills, these seem to be locked in a series of death-defying races. Riding pillion on one of these taxi bikes is a hair-raising experience. Or would be if I hadn't already shaved what I had off.

'Most people who live in Borel,' Catra assured me languidly as we dodged bikes, children, street hawkers and people of complicated sexuality offering diverse personal services, 'are not actual gang members. Many try to make an honest living. Like me.' He grinned. 'The problem? If you live in a favela, everyone assumes you are a criminal before you even open your mouth. The only jobs most honest *favelados* can get in the city are rock-bottom, poorly paid menial stuff like chambermaiding, waiting tables, washing dishes or pumping gas.'

I discovered the truth of this by getting out of bed really early one morning and standing at the bottom of the hill below Borel. Crowds of favela wage slaves swarmed down into the city to work, many in the uniforms of the swanky hotels – the kind I was staying in – which employed them for a pittance. In the evening, as the curtain of tropical darkness falls down hard and fast to close the day, they tread their weary way back home again, sometimes stopping for refreshment on the way up. One of the lasting memories I carried away from Borel is of two respectable-looking middle-aged mothers stopping off at a *boca do fumo* on the way home from work to score a few lines of cocaine. I watched as a couple of armed teenage CV gangsters, one of them clutching a satchel full of ready-wrapped cocaine, perched themselves on a high wall and began trading. In case of trouble the salesmen drop down behind the wall, which offers protection from gunfire. Usually, there will be two or three more gang members either mixing with the customers or sitting somewhere high, watching and ready to defend the *boca* in case of attack.

Joining the end of an orderly queue that formed in a matter of minutes, when it came to their turn the two ladies each handed up the equivalent of two pounds in limp folding money and in return got a small stapled plastic bag holding a gram of cocaine. Leaning on the bonnet of a nearby Volkswagen Beetle, they took out ready-rolled banknotes, stuck them into the bags and snorted heartily. In its own way it was like watching a couple of London matrons stopping off at the local boozer for a stout before heading home to do the chores – except that the cocaine was a lot cheaper. The same amount of coke would cost fifty or sixty pounds in the UK, but in Brazil it generally arrives on the back of a truck, avoiding all those pesky transatlantic shipping and handling costs. Catra assured me the cocaine in Borel is always close to 100 per cent pure – no baking powder, laxative or any other additive padding it out to increase profits as happens elsewhere in the world. I rubbed a smidgen on my lips; they went numb in a matter of seconds.

*

Warned against openly filming drug dealing the next evening, we used a battered nondescript van to do it covertly. Determined to get some footage of the Borel gangs at work, we were in a really dangerous area in the heart of the favela, parked near a well-established *boca*. We got lucky: two very young gangsters arrived, set up shop on top of a nearby wall and began selling cocaine. Punters arrived in ones or twos to get their order, and as soon as we thought we had enough material we stopped filming. Catra had gone off to do some business of his own.

By now, dusk was falling. Assuming everything was cool, I went across the road to get some drinks from a little kiosk. We were standing casually by the van sipping from the cans of soft drink. Mariella, a friend of Fernando who was helping us out that day, was looking past me down a slight slope. We were always very aware of how vulnerable we were, and always on the lookout for trouble, especially near the *bocas*. All of a sudden, Mariella's eyes widened. 'Ross!' She yelled the kind of yell that means life-threatening trouble. Without looking round or even thinking I grabbed her, lifted her up, flung her into the van and leapt in behind her.

When we picked ourselves up again I lifted my head to see why she had shouted. It was an amazing and terrifying sight. Where seconds before the street had been empty, now there were dozens of people breaking in a human tidal wave around the van, rocking it violently from side to side. Word was out the police were mounting a big raid. Terrified in case they missed a fix, the locals were stampeding to the *boca* before that happened. Most raced past on foot, running as hard as they could; others zipped by on scooters and motorbikes; a few people – and this really threw me – charged past on horseback. Whatever their mode of transport, everyone wore the same fixed expression, focused exclusively on the prize up ahead before it disappeared back into the night – and God help anyone who came between them and the drugs. Like us. The police may not have been the problem. This particular *boca* was badly protected, run by a handful of young CV guys. As a result, it often came under attack from rival gangsters.

With a lead on one of the CV gang commanders, once the crowds had passed, Tim, Peter, Fernando and I went further inside the favela on foot, to meet him and his bodyguards. They had agreed to be interviewed on condition we didn't identify them. As darkness fell it started feeling much scarier. 'Night time is gang time,' our contact said right by my ear. 'The favela belongs to the gang.' Paranoid in case we were part of a sting and leading the police in, our guide kept stopping and looking back, dodging left and right through half-finished buildings, doubling back and back again to make sure there was no one on our tail.

By now, it was pitch dark. Our contact led us in through the door of a dilapidated two-storey brick shack. Pointing up, he edged back into the gloom. At the bottom of the stairs, I stopped. Something felt wrong. I went up a few steps to the first turn. A masked face loomed from the darkness above, a pistol pointing straight at my face. Without thinking, I put up my hands. At the same time I felt a surge of anger that blasted out some of the fear. I let my hands fall back to my sides. In a flash contact like this, you trust your gut. And after the initial shock, my gut told me this guy was trying me out: he wanted to see if I would bottle it, fall apart, turn tail and run, beg him not to shoot – whatever. If I had seen something different in his eyes, then run is exactly what I would have done.

I said, 'Don't point that thing at me.' This sounds cool, but I was scared. Anger at being threatened stopped me showing it. Just as well; fear is the worst thing you can let someone see at a time like that. The sentry pointed the semi-automatic away. Beyond him I could see a bare room. Three masked gangsters holding pistols were sitting with their backs against the far wall. One of them had the familiar drug satchel between his knees.

'Come in,' one called softly. 'Join us.' They were jumpy, their eyes flicking over me, then beyond me and back. Under the bandannas pulled up over their noses and mouths, the baseball caps pulled right down, I guessed not one of them was older than eighteen. I went in and squatted down in front of them. The one with the satchel pulled it open. Inside were sixty to seventy standard one-gram cocaine wraps in clear polythene bags stapled carefully closed.

I asked, 'Can I see your weapon?' Without a word, the guy who had spoken handed it over. It was a Ruger 9-millimetre with a full magazine. I checked it; the bullets were live.

Our being alone in the heart of the favela with them worried me; the fact they might have taken drugs worried me; the fact they were armed and so casual with the weapons worried me; but most of all it was their extreme youth and restlessness that set me on edge. I asked the leader how long he expected to live. He shrugged. 'Not too many people make it past their twenties.' Both carrying recent bullet wounds to the legs, his friends to either side of him were living proof of how easy it was to get shot in Borel.

Telling me they wore masks 'because if they see us on the TV, the police will recognize us, come after us and kill us', the boys showed me the hand sign they make to signal membership of Comando Vermelho. *Favelados* who are not actual gangsters make it all the time, even on the dance floor, to confirm their allegiance to the ruling gang.

They stood and led us out through a hatchway onto the flat roof. It was one of the many observation points from where they could spot rival gang or police raids. A Brazilian-manufactured FAL and an early-model Heckler & Koch G3 rifle stood propped against the parapet ready for action. Next thing we knew, someone started firing in our direction. The rounds were coming from some distance, but we could hear bursts of automatic fire. 'You, you go!' someone shouted from the darkness. 'They are shooting at the camera light.' Peter dowsed the light, pronto. I had reached the limits of my bravery for one night.

'OK, let's go, guys,' I shouted. We went – fast.

Next morning, we went back into Borel to do some more filming. It was hot and muggy again, the sky bearing down on us, heavy as lead. Within minutes of leaving the artificial cool of the hotel, my shirt was sticking to my back.

Catra was an expert in the ways of the gangs. *Bocas* like the one we had filmed the day before are continually being attacked by rivals looking to take over. With Rio's internal drugs market alone worth more than £100 million a year and the even bigger international trade on top of that we are talking very large amounts of money – the kind a never-ending stream of gangsters are prepared to fight and die for.

I didn't need Catra to tell me that the relentless fighting is about control of this massively lucrative business. Who controls the favelas controls the drugs trade; who controls the drugs trade gets rich – or at least gets to eat, depending on where a member stands in the rigid gang hierarchy. And it is rigid: at the top is the 'owner', the kingpin who controls trafficking in a whole favela; below him may be one or more general managers, depending on how large and well organized the shanty town is; there is often a product manager who oversees quality control; and then there are the *soldados*, who do the fighting and maintain security, the street dealers, the couriers or 'mules' and finally the lookouts, virtually all of them children.

Everyone, including the top bosses, starts on the bottom rung of the ladder, either as an 'aeroplane' or a lookout. Often as young as six or seven, aeroplanes tout for customers and lead them to the dealers at a *boca do fumo*. Until the 1980s the drug of choice in Brazil was cannabis, with most of the cocaine that came into the country shipped abroad. Since then, more and more of the coke has stayed put in Brazil to supply the burgeoning home market – not least in the favelas themselves – and let's not forget the tourist trade.

Although I had thought they were just kids having fun, Catra gave me the heads-up on the boys flying kites in the stiff onshore breeze. One of the first jobs a wannabe gang member will get is flying a kite to warn the rest of the gang of approaching trouble. The systems differ: sometimes kites flying steadily in a certain area mean everything is cool and dealing can go ahead. If the kites go up in other areas it means police or rival gangsters are on their way, so grab the hardware and get ready to fight. To make sentry duty more interesting, the kids glue ground glass fragments onto the strings of their kites and try to cut one another's lines. Well aware of the part they are playing in the bigger scheme of things, the kids hope that one day, if they live long enough, some of them will reach the top.

But with the average life expectancy of a hard-core gang member in a favela like Borel around nineteen years, they have more chance of winning the lottery. The truth is that most end up dead on garbage heaps. Catra told me about a ten-year-old who showed such promise as a CV colt that he came off the kites after a couple of months and turned to killing. By the time he was twelve, this particular boy had shot dead five men.

By the age of sixteen, many of these boys have children of their own. More often than not, these kids will join the family business in their turn. What's life without something to hand on to your offspring? Trailing death, crime and disorder in their wake, Rio's gangsters burn fast and short. Whatever they might start out doing for the gang, if they follow the usual career path and move up through the ranks to become *soldados*, by the time they are teenagers they will generally have made their first hit – killing a rival gangster, a traitor or a customer who has made a life-threatening mistake like trying to cheat the gang or failing to pay a debt. On their way, they will have committed armed robberies, extortion and a whole host of other crimes. Catra said most Rio gang chapters operate an iron rule of 'blood in, blood out' – you have to kill to join, and you have to die to leave. In between, if you are not selling drugs then what you mostly do is kill.

In the favelas, death is casual and dying is everyday.

So while they might be colourful, vibrant and fascinating to the point where some of the bigger and better developed ones have started admitting thrill-seeking tourists for a small fee, we need to remember that favelas are very, very deadly places. Being a fully paid-up gangster in an area like Borel means fighting war to the death, day in and day out, with serious firepower: 7.62-millimetre FAL self-loading rifles, Heckler & Koch G3s with enough power to punch through the shell of a car and kill its occupants, RPG-7 armour-piercing rocket-propelled grenades, hand grenades – they use a lot of these – SPAS-12 shotguns, landmines. You name it, the gangsters either already have it or they can buy it at will.

With this sort of weaponry and plenty of willing *soldados* to use it, CV, Amigos dos Amigos and the Terceiro Comando (TC) can and do take on Brazil's CORE (special police commando) units as and when. The police in their turn dare only go into the favelas mob-handed, with top cover in the form of helicopters and squads of commandos able to fast-rope in, hunt down a target and either pluck him out or kill him. If they are lucky, that is, and they put down enough firepower; if a RPG-7 round or a burst from a heavy machine gun doesn't hit the helicopter and if the snatch squads succeed. When they do go in, the resulting shoot-outs are like something out of a Western, as the police video footage we were given of one such battle shows. Waged over rooftops and through twisting, narrow alleyways, during this firefight one policeman and two CV gang members died.

To make it harder for the police the gangs work mainly at night, using the rooftops to travel, taking to the streets only as a last resort. The police wear masks or hoods; like the gangsters they hunt, many of them live in the favelas, heading off to work every day in civilian clothes and then changing into uniform at their police station. If the gangs ever got to know what they did for a living, most of these officers would be dead within the day. Living in the favelas they are trying to police, they certainly know the turf. No one on either side plays by any rules. The gangs kill policemen, civilians and anyone who gets in their way without a second thought. For their part, some police and CORE members hand out summary justice, including on-the-spot execution, torture and imprisonment without trial. Thanks to the efforts of our local fixer, Fernando, we were lucky enough to obtain footage of one police squad dragging a suspected dealer they had just arrested behind a bus. The shooting that follows does little to suggest he stayed alive.

The godfathers who run the favelas do sometimes live in them; if you are wanted by the law, then burrowed deep inside the likes of the Morro do Borel is the safest place to be. But increasingly the very top bosses live surrounded by armed bodyguards in fortified mansions in the better parts of the city, or in Florida. They pull the narco-strings, take the cash and let the gang manage business on the streets. A handful of people make a huge amount of money, and everybody else just gets by. I saw no mansions in the favelas – only clusters of crummy, low-rise blocks.

The violence that dogs the cities of Brazil isn't all that surprising. Moving between my pleasant First World hotel and a Third World shanty in the space of a single day, I could see that the gap between the city's rich and poor could hardly be greater. Or any more shocking. The large numbers of wealthy foreign tourists who come for the sex trade, to soak up some of the exotic atmosphere and for the natural beauty of the place add fuel to the social fire, as does the violent legacy of the generals who ruled the place with bullets and blood for so many years.

As with almost every controlling organization in the world, identity is all-important to Rio's warring criminal gangs. Gang colours, gang graffiti – it is all about belonging to the group, the extended gang family, the substitute for hearth and home and family life that most of the people who join the gangs have never known. In the Rio favelas red is the colour of CV, while TC flaunts shades of green. The graffiti is a turf marker; the tags set the borderlines warning rival gangs to steer clear. Murals can put an ironic twist on the everyday reality of favela life, even depicting a stereotypical drug dealer supplying a white customer.

The Borel *favelados* are intelligent, articulate and very politically aware. In fact, many favela gang members use the massive inequality in Brazilian society to justify taking on the rich ruling elite, portraying themselves as latter-day Robin Hoods. When I got him on this subject, Catra waxed eloquent. 'The favela protects itself,' he told me. 'The ordinary person as well as the drugs trafficker needs protection. Society attacks us and keeps us in a corner. We are in a civil war.'

The first serious gang in the city, Catra said, Comando Vermelho was formed in the 1970s to take on the vicious right-wing junta then in power. As well as using torture on its real or imagined opponents as a matter of routine, the junta made the mistake of locking up charismatic, intelligent left-wing agitators and rebels with ordinary criminals. From this enforced cell-block mix came a strange hybrid animal: the radical, politically self-justifying criminal gangs that rule Rio's favelas today, using the have/have-not gulf to justify taking on the rich, the police and the establishment. In reality, the Robin Hood stuff in which the gangsters like to cloak themselves is almost wholly undeserved. Every gang makes money from the proceeds of drugs and violent crime, and its *soldados* will kill anyone at any time to defend its interests. Coming in as an outsider, I found it hard to spot any social justice at work in the mess.

The gangs may not be stealing from the rich to give to the poor, but they do throw a great party. Everybody in Brazil likes to dance, and that includes gangsters. A man has to let his hair down after work, especially when it's such a stressful business. As in all wars, the ever-present prospect of death makes people party all the harder. I could hardly tour Borel with one of its most famous sons without trying one. Catra led me to a long, low-ceilinged shack, one of the hottest, sweatiest rooms I have ever been in. It was a barely contained riot. A very important part of favela life, *baile funk* is kind of extreme-gangsta-rap-meets-techno-salsa. Heavy on the drums, it combines sexually explicit lyrics sung at a shout with throbbing bass lines and melodies ripped and looped from other people's songs. *Baile funk* fuels the riotous favela dance scene, the sweatiest, noisiest, sexiest disco you will ever visit in your entire life.

Most of the people shaking their stuff were teenagers, and only the guys on the door were armed. MC Catra grabbed the mike and got to work, his first song being a long, graphic rap about having lots of sex. Swigging Skol, smoking dope and taking a variety of other substances, frequently all at the same time, everyone cheered at the chorus, which encouraged them to have more and more exotic sex. After a couple of numbers, the wild dancing made the room even hotter and people started to strip. Since they weren't wearing much to begin with, this meant that at least half of the women in the crowd were down to their dental floss.

I was just getting into the swing of it when Catra stopped the music. Pointing at the shaven-headed English guy, he told the crowd I was going to make a speech. The bastard. With the whole place clapping and cheering, and the prospect of summary execution if I failed to oblige, I stepped up to the microphone.

I told the sweating, heaving mob how pleased I was to be in Borel, what a great crowd they were and how nice it was of them to let me join in the fun. I'm not sure how many of them understood a word of what I said, but when I stopped speaking they all cheered wildly once more, Catra started the music off again, and everyone got back down to the business of having a good time. I was just glad they hadn't opened fire.

Next stop, on our third day, was Cantagalo favela, which is loosely controlled by CV's most serious opposition, TC. It smelled of the usual things: car oil, diesel fumes from the hundreds of generators used to provide power, sewage, cooking smoke, marijuana and rotting rubbish. The river that ran through the settlement was so polluted and toxic that any kids who fell into the water had to be fished out super fast, and even then they were at risk of serious illness.

As in all the favelas we visited there was a continuous background din, a mixture of *baile funk* blasting out from competing dance venues, gunfire, shouting, clapping and the revving of scooters and small motorbikes. Any newish cars you see in a favela have been stolen from the city by gang members, and once they are in, they don't come back out. Would you go into a favela to retrieve your stolen motor? Me neither.

In baseball caps, dark glasses and with T-shirts wrapped up and over their heads leaving only their eyes showing, the five TC gang members we'd arranged to meet had the weapons handling skills of not very intelligent two-year-olds. They were also passing round a joint. As soon as they saw the camera they started larking about and showing off, pointing their guns and striking Rambo-style poses. If they hadn't all been extremely young, drugged up, with their index fingers wrapped around the triggers and the safety catches off, this might have been funny. Nothing makes me more nervous than drugged teenagers waving loaded firearms in my face, and this lot were the worst I had so far seen. Even in the best-disciplined military units, accidents happen. The chances of one now were off the scale, and I didn't want to be on the end of it.

We crabbed towards them, keeping a wary eye on the weapons. I asked them what would happen if CV came into Cantagalo. They started laughing uncontrollably, the first setting off the next and then back along the line again, cackling away like hyenas. Next thing we knew they were staging a mock gunfight for the camera, showing us how it was done – correction, showing us how *they* did it. This made me want to find the nearest ditch and lie flat on my face until they had stopped. When they finally grew tired of posing we managed to talk a little, but even our translator, Fernando, found it hard to make sense of their slurred, addled sentences. But he found out the reason the boys couldn't stop laughing – as well as smoking dope, they had just popped their first Ecstasy pills.

One thing the gang were very clear about was the

punishment they meted out to informers. First, and while the victim was still alive, they sliced off his arms and legs; then they slowly sawed off his head; and, as a final flourish, they threw the bits into a shallow grave, doused them in petrol and burned them. Called the 'microwave', they said the point of this last bit was to show disrespect to the informant's family, especially his mother. They also believed that if they dismembered the person, that is how he would remain in the afterlife. While he told me all this, the gold cross on the gang leader's chest winked in the dim favela light.

This kind of treatment isn't just handed out to informers; anyone deemed to have shown TC disrespect stands to get it. On 3 June 2003 TV Globo reporter Tim Lopes, who had already made a programme about Rio's gangs that suggested some of them were involved in the sexual abuse of minors, made the mistake of entering a favela to do a follow-up. A group of gangsters caught Lopes, tortured him, cut off his arms and legs while he was still alive, sliced off his head and then gave what was left of him the microwave.

Unable to get any more coherent comments out of them as the Ecstasy took hold, I thanked the gang for sharing their experiences. With a final flourish of their weapons, they turned and slipped off back into the darkness.

Keen to see how much truth there was in the supposed political origins of the CV, I next went to visit an intriguing man named William da Silva Lima in Rio's central prison. Imprisoned as a young student under the junta on a charge of armed robbery, da Silva Lima is known to his admirers as 'the professor'. Lima is widely seen and respected as the guru and founding father of Comando Vermelho. He too has his war wounds: during his time inside, a warder beat him over the head with a shovel. He survived the attack – but only just. He also managed to escape from prison twice, but was each time recaptured. When I met him, da Silva Lima was only three weeks away from release after thirty-six years in jail.

From what I had seen, I told him, it seemed that CV is more about help yourself than self-help. He replied with the same rebel gleam in his eye that must have helped get him arrested in the first place, 'We set up Comando Vermelho not as a criminal gang but as a means of fighting for social and economic justice. For the people. And for the first years, it *was* about the people. Now,' he shook his head, 'it's just another gang selling drugs on the streets.' I felt sad; it must be very, very tough to see your idealistic dream of a fairer society go up in a bonfire of crime.

To get another view of Rio's biggest problem I went to see Vera Malaguti. I needed to meet some people on the right side of the law, people who were trying to make a difference. A criminologist who has written extensively about the gangs, Malaguti has a pleasant bungalow in a vibrant green, sub-rainforest suburb that sits in a gully between two favelas. As we spoke the sound of gunfire crackled around and above us. 'Don't worry,' she said with miraculous calm, 'it's just Santa Marta – that favela over there.' She pointed over her garden fence. 'They're shooting it out with their neighbour on the other side.' It beats arguments over fences and hedges. I tried hard not to worry about the whizzing lead.

Her tone was calm and even, given what she was telling me. 'Twelve hundred young poor black kids are killed by the Rio police every year and fifty million Brazilians live below the poverty line.' The sound of high-velocity rounds in the background helped me believe her every word. Vera's main point is that Brazil has a class system much more rigid even than Britain's at its worst. 'It is not just that 10 per cent of Brazil's population owns 80 per cent of the country's wealth; it's that there is no movement across or between the classes. Everything is fixed; everything stays in the same place – the poor in their favela ghettos and the rich in their walled and guarded compounds. Which are also ghettos, only with running water, electricity, servants and satellite TV.' She compressed her lips. 'The police are there to make sure it stays that way: they protect the rich, and themselves. That's it. But what we really have going on in Brazil is civil war.'

After hearing what Malaguti had to say, I went down to meet some of the CORE special weapons and assault teams. In part trained by US DEA and SWAT experts, the CORE guys are a very macho crew. They are very proud of what they do, and use the same kind of striking, death-laden imagery as Rio's actual gangs – only stronger. There was definitely no hanging back when it came to the shields and badges plastered onto their black uniforms. A typical example? A lurid skull and crossbones with a dagger piercing one eye, a syringe spearing the other and a big rifle behind all that in case you still hadn't quite got the message. And if you believed Malaguti, then all the pirate symbolism was apt.

Some of the crew are specially selected for their shortness – those who act as door gunners on the compact four-seat helicopters used for airborne assaults. In a cramped cabin filled with weapons, ammo and their hulking fellow CORE assault commandos space is at a premium, and the less of it a door gunner takes up the better. One man, a veteran of many shoot-outs, had a prosthetic left forearm complete with metal Dr No-style pincers fitted after a heavy-calibre round had blown away the original. Dr No had a Glock 17 strapped to the top of his right thigh, a .38 Smith & Wesson revolver on his left boot, plus steel handcuffs and plasticuffs looped on his belt. This along with smoke grenades, flash-bang assault grenades and pepper spray. One big serrated-edge combat knife was holstered across the front of his flak jacket. Another was strapped to his left arm, a flick knife concealed in one pocket, and a large number of spare magazines for his pistol and M16 assault rifle were draped across his chest. A stand-out member of Rio's CORE squad, he looked more like a cross between the Terminator and Long John Silver than a police officer.

Speaking of Dr No, when they go in to extract a favela gang leader, which is the airborne commandos' speciality, they do it in classic pincer style. The helicopters with their fast-rope special weapons attack teams come in over the target while armoured personnel carriers and accompanying teams bully up through the slums from the bottom of the hill. The police hope either to catch or kill the villains trapped somewhere in the middle. When they see the drug dealers run, the helicopter gunners start shooting, obviously taking very special care not to harm any innocent *favelados* who might happen to stray into their sights.

My next interview was with Rodrigo Oliveira, head of the DRE, Brazil's anti-drug unit. One of the best cops I've ever met – and I've met a few – Oliveira showed me his .45-inch (11.43-millimetre) Glock 37 GAP pistol. Most Glocks chamber a 9-millimetre round but, as Oliveira put it, 'If I shoot someone, I only want to have to shoot them once, not twice.' Fair enough. Trained in the US by the DEA and the FBI, Oliveira was one of the most open officials I have met, readily admitting what the gangsters had already told us. The police weren't always part of the solution in Rio; some of them were part of the problem. It was true, Oliveira told us cheerfully: many of the police kidnapped gangsters, drove them down to Ipanema,

Leblon or Copacabana and held them in a hotel for a few days until the ransom money – usually about $30,000 – arrived from their family and/or fellows. And if the money didn't arrive, who could say what happened?

Looping in a police helicopter over Rocinha, South America's largest shanty town and home to an estimated 150,000 people, Oliveira admitted it was controlled by CV. Kidnap and extortion, he said, are a way of life there as they are in all the favelas. 'That's the way it has always been, the way it is and the way it always will be.' He said that if a top Brazilian footballer happens to be unmarried and have no children available for abduction, then gangsters will kidnap his mother. Faced with bits of Mum arriving in the post, most loving sons pay up. Given this state of affairs, many mothers of Rio's rich and famous now do their shopping with a couple of armed ex-special forces men close by. It works out cheaper in the long run, and you don't have the stress of kidnap.

Another thing that goes on, according to a woman we ran into as we were watching the CORE fast-rope attack teams go through their formidable paces earlier that day, is that elements in the police will sometimes work in conjunction with a gang to take over a given favela, then take a slice of the drug-selling pie ever after. All hard to prove, but this particular woman told us that in the course of one of these attempted takeovers, it was the police who had shot and wounded her. She certainly bore the scars of multiple bullet wounds.

Having spent a few days in their company, I thought there were plenty of Rio police officers trying to do the right thing, including most of the CORE guys who allowed us to film them at work, but that this good work was being undermined by a significant minority bent on lining their pockets through extra-curricular activities like kidnapping gang leaders and holding them for ransom. This, Vera Malaguti had told me, is a very common way for bent policemen to bump up their salaries. Since these amount on average to less than $200 a month, the fact that some of them stray from the path of righteousness isn't all that surprising.

As a kind of final treat CORE invited us to inspect the arsenal of weapons it had seized from gangs. Housed in a heavily fortified warehouse the size of a football pitch and protected 24/7 by armed guards, the Fantoni weapons store forms part of Rio Central police station. Stuffed from floor to ceiling with rifles, hand-guns, grenades, rocket launchers, shotguns and machine guns of every age, origin and in every condition from brand new, still embalmed in their factory grease, to antique, this was an amazing place. A kind of British Library for weapons; every time you turned a corner there were more. Every single one of the 85,000 weapons there, the custodian told me proudly, was in working order; every single one of them could still be used to kill.

The biggest collection of lethal weaponry I had ever seen in one place, and most likely ever will, there was enough hardware in there to start a small war. But what was it for? When I asked a custodian, 'Why haven't you destroyed all these weapons so they don't end up back on the street?' he replied with a knowing smile, 'What if we need them to fight the gangs?' I don't think so. The word on the street is the weapons are stored for later sale, perhaps back to the gangsters the police took them from in the first place, perhaps elsewhere. The attitude seemed to be, 'Weapons are valuable – why destroy a chance for profit?' The Rio police were certainly in a war but its moral battle lines struck me as fluid.

My next stop was Rio's notorious Polinter remand prison. I had heard this was a terrible place – and as the facility where many gangsters ended up I wanted to see it – but the reality still shocked me to the bone. Cameras are generally forbidden in Polinter; the authorities are too embarrassed to let the outside world see what goes on inside. But the fact that we went in with a group of evangelical Christians who had a regular gig at the jail helped us bypass the usual restrictions.

Once through the initial security checks, we found ourselves at a door guarded by two warders armed with pump-action sawn-offs. Assuming we were part of the missionary flock they gave us the nod through, but they reminded us that once we were inside the prison proper we were on our own. There are no warders in the cell blocks, and if we got into trouble no one would come to our immediate aid. We moved through the door, turned right into a low, fetid corridor and walked in.

It was like a battery farm for humans, except that on the chicken farm where I once worked the birds had more individual space, more light and more air. Imagine an underground car park packed full of metal cages. The floors, walls and ceiling grey concrete streaked with brown stains. The heat, humidity and lack of oxygen stifling. One hundred and fifty inmates crammed in cages designed for fifteen. Hundreds of men in conditions that make Death Row look comfortable, huddled and crouched in long rows, arms stretching vainly through the bars. Men with no beds, forced to take turns sleeping in rough hammocks fashioned out of trousers and shirts tied together with belts. Men with no toilets, forced to urinate into drinks bottles and defecate into plastic shopping bags. When these are full they either wedge them between the bars or tie them there with string. Rows of these bottles and bags filled with raw human excrement line the cage walls, making the smell in there so bad you could carve it. All prisoners have to buy their own plastic bags. If they have no money and try to excrete on the floor, their cellmates literally kick the shit out of them. In Polinter you either have money to start with or you sell yourself to get it.

Mixed with that toilet stink was the sharp musk of massed, sweating bodies, the burned smell of badly cooked meat and something else that I could not, perhaps did not want to, identify. The heat was so intense the sweat from the hundreds of unwashed bodies condensed on the low roof and dripped back down to the floor. Before going in, we had been warned not to look up; there was a high risk of catching an eye infection. Dysentery, HIV/Aids and other diseases are rife.

With so many men packed into such a small space, the wardens let the prisoners police themselves. In practice, this means the weakest inmates go to the wall: bullied, beaten, sexually abused and made to serve the stronger men. Peter, the cameraman, saw one dark cage filled with what seemed like naked men. One man was on top of another, holding him from behind. He could hardly believe it. No one even cared that there was a cameraman right there. Peter joined us and said in a low, shocked voice, 'Look at that bloke – he's got an arsehole the size of a tennis ball.' I looked and wished I hadn't; it was true. As we passed them, mixed in with the rest of the men, the 'ladyboy' transvestites shouted catcalls and pulled their tight cut-off jeans aside to flaunt their backsides. Some men were lying flat out on the cage floors. They looked unconscious.

I met the prison governess. When I asked if the men ever had a shower, she shook her head. 'The only thing I can do is get a fire hose in here from time to time and wash the cages out. They are happy for it.' Gazing at the crouched, stinking hordes, I could well believe it. Anything to break up the horrible day. Anything to help reduce the filth.

Ecstatic to be out of their cages, the few dozen lucky prisoners selected to attend the evangelical roadshow sat in docile rows like a bunch of schoolkids. I watched as their eyes slid constantly to the preacher's team of lady assistants. Wearing full-length, shiny, bright-blue imitation-silk dresses, the female chorus clapped and swayed and sang in time to the loud gospel music, endorsing their leader's shouted exhortations to renounce evil and take the straight and narrow path. The prisoners liked it best when the choir swayed.

More than just a literally captive audience, some of the prisoners were enlisted in the elaborate show that now took place. The preacher, Pastor Marcos, was an imposing, charismatic figure with a bouffant hairdo and a shiny suit who reminded me strongly of soul brother number one, James Brown. Marcos called an evil-looking inmate with a vicious, hangdog look about him out of the crowd. Chanting what sounded to my ear like magic spells or talking tongues, the pastor placed a hand on the prisoner's bony close-shaven skull and ordered the 'devils' inside him to come out.

On cue, the chosen man's limbs began to jerk and twitch, his eyes rolled towards the ceiling and his gaze became distant, unfocused. Shaking in every limb, he crashed to the floor and had what looked like an epileptic fit. Great spasms racked his muscles. He spun on his back like a breakdancer, flipped, thrashed like a fish; he spun on his face, pushing his front teeth right through his lower lip. The preacher stepped back to

46

avoid the flailing feet. At last the prisoner jumped up and a beatific smile appeared on his face. The pastor patted him as if he were a dog, then, raising both arms to heaven, he announced in ringing tones that the prisoner was cured.

Was this all an act – a carefully staged show rehearsed in advance? I doubt it. The men in the room believed in the pastor. Shouting 'Glory to Jehovah' at the tops of their voices, every one of them seemed convinced that a miracle had taken place and evil spirits had been driven from the heart of a man. The applause kept on going, resounding off the bare walls. The swearing pastor beamed and his followers clapped, swayed and sang, the blue shiny stuff of their dresses reflecting the uncertain light. There was a feeling of hysteria, a strong sense that everyone had to join in – or else. I clapped along with the best of them; standing out seemed unwise. With just a few warders in with us and none of them armed, the last thing you wanted was to upset the crowd.

Pastor Marcos exorcized a second prisoner, whose expurgation was if anything even more convincing and dramatic than the first. Then he beckoned me forward. Oh, oh. With every eyeball in the place fixed on me, I could hardly refuse. Placing a large, sweaty hand on my scalp, he pushed my head back with sharp, powerful jerks that in the intense heat and supercharged atmosphere made me feel disoriented. 'Devil begone!' he shouted. 'Devil begone!' The pastor said he felt the presence of bad spirits inside me, but as he went through his prayers and incantations and his cleansing routine I felt nothing other than dizziness from being pushed around. I was also even sweatier than before, a thing I could not have believed possible. Dredging up a performance, I put on a show of being cleansed, although many of my friends would say the pastor didn't quite work his magic.

Why do the prison authorities conspire and collude in such performances? Well, for a start it helps keep the prisoners quiet. Evangelical Baptist missionaries are gaining a lot of power in modern Brazil – odd in a country that has for so long been so Catholic. In this jail they seemed able to turn up when they pleased and do as they liked with the inmates.

If you join a gang, the chances are you will wind up somewhere like Polinter.

The final break of the trip was an invitation which came through the usual murky channels to go back into Borel and meet one of the CV main players. A trail of late-night meetings led us deep into the favela. I was conscious that, as before, the gangsters were checking us out the whole time to see if there was any sign of a set-up with the police. Paranoid about getting caught – and wouldn't you be with the prospect of Polinter – the gangsters insisted we could only go in as a skeleton crew: cameraman Peter, Heron on sound, Tim and me. We waited in the dark. A short, skinny youth with a bandanna pulled up over his nose stepped out of the night. 'Stay with me,' he warned, then turned and slipped back into the warren of lanes. Lithe as a cat, he moved quickly over the rough ground. We hurried after him like Alice after the White Rabbit. Again and again our guide doubled and redoubled back on his tracks, up, down, left and right, twisting and turning to make sure no one was on our tail.

After four hours of this we reached a tumbledown brick shack. By now it was past one in the morning, and except for a distant, thumping bass most of the noise had subsided. The man ushered us down some stairs and disappeared without a word. The place was hot, stuffy and looked dirt poor. Two old people, a man and a woman, peered at us. I tried to say hello in Portuguese, but the word stuck in my throat. The couple were amazed to see us, even more surprised than we were to arrive unannounced. They stared at us as if we had just stepped off a spaceship. For an odd moment I felt as if they were the real observers here in the night, and not us with our probing camera.

They gave us a Skol and we waited. I glanced around. A single bare light bulb hung from the low ceiling. There was a rickety sideboard, a Calor gas stove, a table and two chairs. In the adjoining room I glimpsed a low home-made wooden bed, a bucket in the corner for the necessary. Then a phone call came through from Fernando waiting back at the *boca do fumo*: 'They are on their way.' Adrenalin surged into my blood and I woke up. This was the real deal – the CV's head guys. If they took against us, if we had to split up and run, I knew I would never get back out, at least not in one piece. We were too far inside, the path we had taken too confusing.

We heard soft footfalls on the roof above. Men dropped down into the alleyway outside and then they were in the room. Five gang members. The first had a FAL self-loading rifle he kept cradled like an infant to his chest, the second a pump-action shotgun; all had automatic pistols held at the ready. One of them had the biggest satchel of drugs I had so far seen hung around his shoulder. They were all masked, two of them in T-shirts pulled up over their heads leaving only a gap for the eyes, the others in baseball caps or beanies pulled down low and bandannas. As far as I could tell, none of them was more than twenty years old.

Patting his rifle, the gang leader told me, 'This is my best friend. I got three kids, and I have to look after them.' He said the police were just another gang on the take, involved in kidnapping for ransom, extortion, selling firearms and a whole range of other illegal ways of increasing their income. When I challenged this, he glared at me. 'Listen,' he said softly. 'The police came to my house in the night and kidnapped *me*. And then demanded a ransom. "Either you give us drugs or money. Or we give you to the Amigos dos Amigos."'

He said his elder brother had been shot by the Amigos dos Amigos, and more than twenty of his friends had also died at the hands of the police or rival gangs. 'I am at war with the Amigos dos Amigos and with the police because they are corrupt. ADA are mixed up with the police. That's why we have to fight them. We die at the hands of cowards, cut into pieces. I sleep with this gun. It is my other arm; it protects me. First God, then my gun.'

After we had talked, they asked us to join them for a drink. Some girls turned up. A couple of long cold Skols later, the gangsters decided they wanted to dance. The leader handed me his rifle and asked if I'd hold it while he took to the floor. His deputy passed me his pump-action shotgun. So there I sat, with a Remington shotgun across my lap, a Skol and a cigarette in one hand and a self-loading rifle in the other, watching the Borel CV head honchos having fun.

The next morning I packed and made ready to leave. Checking out, I handed my credit card to the receptionist to pay my minibar bill. The man swiped the card, handed it back to me and off I went. Ivan arrived in his cab to drive me back to the airport and a cold grey London. 'What did you learn about the gangs?' he asked, picking up our conversation from my first day in Rio three weeks ago. 'When I was a kid, we used to play cops and robbers, swing in trees and if we did fight we fought with our fists. At the most we used sticks and stones. But not here.' He shook his head. 'No. Here, the kids do not play at war. The crime is for real and they use only guns.' My feelings were mixed as we spooled back out north along the Gaza Strip towards Galeao Antonio Carlos Jobim International. I loved the warmth and immediacy of Rio's people, but hated the crushing poverty and the murderous gangs.

We had to change at São Paulo, 200 miles to the south-west. The flight lasted two hours. I was sitting there congratulating myself on the fact that I hadn't been mugged or otherwise done over during my time in Rio but the city still had a surprise in store for me. As soon as we landed I turned on my mobile phone as usual in case of messages. There was a text from my bank: 'Please call immediately.' I was still on the plane but I called. 'Excuse our asking, Mr Kemp,' said a polite English voice on the other end of the line, 'but we were wondering how you managed to spend so much money in the last two hours.'

'Excuse *me*,' I shot back, 'but I've been in the air for the last two hours. The only thing that should be on that card since I left Rio is a hotel minibar bill for fifty dollars.'

'No, Mr Kemp. Since leaving Rio you have spent more than £12,000.'

'Twelve thousand pounds?' I shouted. 'Kill the card! Kill the card!' There is already far too much killing in Brazil but this particular fatality could not come fast enough.

'We'll do that at once, sir, of course,' said the soft voice on the other end, 'but we think your card has been cloned, possibly more than once. People have been spending on it all over Rio de Janeiro and surrounding districts.'

By the time we landed at Heathrow eight hours later the total had gone up to more than £23,000. I wasn't charged but the moral of the story is, when in Rio pay your bills in cash if you can, because a lot of the locals see a gringo's credit card as a meal ticket. You have to work really hard to spend £23,000 in a couple of hours in Rio de Janeiro. I hope they enjoyed it.

Brazilians are obsessed with football — and world-beaters as a result. In the favelas the kids play all the time, racing after plastic footballs in the mud or the dust. Through Peter the cameraman we had met a local man who did not want to be named but who worked for a charity that tried to stop favela children joining the gangs. He told me what the kids needed most was team shirts, so they knew whose side they were on when they played soccer.

When I got back to the hotel that evening I had called Reebok and asked if they would maybe give the kids some shirts. Reebok came up trumps, promising to supply a few sets for free. Back in London three weeks later, I rang to see if the shirts had arrived. 'They have arrived,' said the man. 'Many thanks for that.' There was an awkward pause, the kind that tells you something is badly wrong.

'Are the shirts OK?' I asked.

'The shirts are very good,' he said. 'Thank you. But three of the kids you saw playing that day have been shot dead.'

Shortly after we left Rio the gangs came back to town. In a series of coordinated attacks launched just after dawn on 28 December 2006, mobs of favela gangsters attacked more than twenty police stations with hand grenades and automatic weapons. Smashing windows and looting shops in Rio's smarter areas, the gangsters hijacked six of the city's buses, stripping the terrified passengers of their valuables. One mob went further: jamming shut its doors, they set fire to a bus, trapping seven people inside. The passengers burned to death. In total, twenty-one people died that day, including two policemen. Given the scale of the violence, the only miracle was that the toll of death and injury was not even higher. It wasn't the first time the gangs had reminded the authorities of their awesome power, and as long as the gap between Brazil's rich and poor remains as wide as it is, it won't be the last.

2. New Zealand

A country with ten times more sheep than it has people, you would expect New Zealand to be quiet. And on the whole it is, at least if the people outside Wellington railway station were anything to go by. They looked well behaved and civilized, skirting the neat flower beds on either side of the square as they went about their lawful business. The area around the handsome terminus had a distinct retro feel, as if New Zealand's capital was ticking over twenty years in the past. It felt much gentler and sleepier than the London I had left a day or two earlier – quaint in the nicest possible way. A good place to live, I thought, if you like a clean outdoor life and a spot of peace.

But this country has more gangs per head than any other country in the world, and two of the worst, the Mongrel Mob and Black Power, are locked in a deadly battle to be top dog. This conflict, which has been going on for decades, affects even the quietest and otherwise most pleasant towns and cities of these beautiful islands. And nowhere is this more true than in the town of Wairoa. A small and beautiful community of some 5,000 people on Hawke Bay which is on the east coast of North Island, when I went up to take a look at it Wairoa was New Zealand as I had always imagined: quiet, clean, attractive, well kept – just like the country's capital. Except for the local gangs: for three decades and more Wairoa has been dogged by some of New Zealand's worst violence.

In one of the biggest fights, large numbers of Black Power and Mongrel Mobsters gathered outside Wairoa District Court in November 2002. A local Mongrel Mob member was on trial for the alleged assault of a Black Power rival. With large numbers of opposing gangsters milling around the courthouse, this was a stick of dynamite waiting for a match. The gangs traded insults. And then it came to blows. The knives and the motorcycle chains came out, then the guns. And after that all hell let loose.

The fighting exploded out of the courthouse and raged down Wairoa's main street, sending innocent citizens scurrying for cover. It was like a scene from a Western movie. By the time the battle ended, two men lay dead, one stabbed and a second shot. Outnumbered by at least a dozen to one, the Wairoa police called neighbouring forces for help. Dozens of gangsters were rounded up and sent for trial on charges ranging from affray to murder. In the most serious case the prosecution alleged that two Mongrel Mobsters acting on the suggestion of a third had lain in wait near the courthouse and then shot dead Henry William Waihape, aged twenty-nine, a passenger in a Black Power vehicle. More than a dozen Mongrel Mobsters and sixteen Black

Power gang members were convicted on various charges relating to the fight. All bar a couple went to prison.

In an earlier but no less notorious case a man named Mahi Kamona had his stomach cut out in an attack that almost cost him his life. A Wairoa citizen not in either gang, Kamona saw a group of Mongrel Mobsters mistreating some of the town's girls. He stepped in to try to protect them. The Mobsters set about him, but Kamona, who is not a small man, gave better than he got and punched one of his assailants unconscious. A few minutes later more Mongrel Mobsters came looking for revenge. Sergeant Chris Flood of the Wairoa police can't forget what he saw when he responded to the emergency call: 'We were called to the New Wairoa Hotel. We arrived there and sure enough in the toilet block of the hotel there was a guy who had been stabbed. It was more than a stabbing; he had almost been disembowelled.'

For Kamona, the memories are no less vivid. 'I can remember it like it happened just ten minutes ago. I'd just had a piss. I turned around, pulling up the zip, opened the door to walk out and as you are opening up the door the knives are going straight into your guts. You are trying to pull your zip up and there is a blade going straight in and coming out.'

Flood said, 'His intestines were coming out and we just kind of held them there . . . We got bar towels. I couldn't believe what I was seeing, that someone had done something like that to somebody else.'

At home in his living room, Kamona lifted his T-shirt to show me the scars of his injuries. The attackers had really sliced him up: the flesh was pocked and contorted, with thick ridges, welts and broad white stitch marks from the cuts and the repairs that had saved his life. 'Just a few cuts,' Kamona told me, trying to play it cool, but when I asked him what it was like to live with the injuries, he looked away. 'There's no muscles in there to keep your stomach there.' He kept saying 'your' as if the terrible injuries had happened to someone else.

Here I was waiting to meet members of the Mongrel Mob outside Wellington station on my first morning in New Zealand. I glanced up the street. They were more than an hour late. I was just thinking we'd need to rearrange the meeting when a long cream-coloured customized Cadillac town car with a magenta contrast paint job swerved out of the passing traffic and slid to a stop beside me. In case of any doubt about its status, the Caddy's number plate read PIMP ON.

The nearside rear door swung open, and one of the three men inside told me to get in. For a few seconds I hesitated – and not just on account of the lurid purple dashboard and interior trim. The men had heavy tattoos on their faces that made them look like they were wearing masks. In fact, that's what a full facial tattoo is called over there. One of them was also wearing a Nazi coal scuttle helmet complete with chinstrap and swastikas. All three wore 'reggies' or 'originals' – evil-smelling, never-been-washed denim jeans and waist-coats plastered with red and black Mongrel Mob gang patches. They were the kind of people you wouldn't want to meet in the back of a Cadillac. Or a dark alley. Or even a very brightly lit alley. Everything about them said, 'We are the Mongrel Mob. Fuck off.'

I got in. The Mongrels decorate their faces, club-houses and clothing with brash, cartoon-style bulldog emblems – their gang logo, like a corporate identity. The man at the wheel had bulldog images all over his face and body. They were jumbled up with words and other symbols I couldn't at first decipher. In case any-one hadn't already got the message from the bulldogs, MOBSTER was drilled in soot black on a red ground across the driver's forehead. A stiff Mohican of black hair gave him extra height. Shaved to the bone, both sides of his long head displayed two more of the tattooed bulldogs, their tongues sticking right out. His fists and arms were tattooed, and the pictures covering his face ran on down his neck below the edge of his T-shirt. He wore a wide black leather and steel wrist cuff on his right forearm, a Confederate flag bandanna round his neck, and when he stood on the gas pedal I noticed he was barefoot. His appearance and the extra edge of menace in his gaze marked this man out as Dennis Makalio, the man who was going to tell me the secrets of the Mongrel Mob, one of New Zealand's most notorious gangs. Or the man who might just turn in his seat, punch me in the face and throw me out of the window with his free hand. Like his mates, he was easily strong enough.

Nobody said anything. Gangsters don't do introductions. Staring at these guys, and it was hard not to, I thought, in short order, What have I let myself in for? Why have I come to do this? and I must be insane.

A Mongrel Mob elder statesman, Makalio was a very scary guy. Right away I saw that on this first meeting he didn't like the look of me any more than I did of him. I was just beginning to wonder if we were going to get a programme out of this visit at all when our director, Jonathan Jones, JJ, stepped in. We had driven over to my hotel and had met JJ outside. Why didn't Makalio and I go in and have a drink? he suggested. Well, it was better than staring. But what JJ and I didn't know was that going for a drink with Dennis Makalio wasn't quite as easy as that. Mongrel Mob gangsters are barred from all of New Zealand's hotels, and only the roughest bars will serve them. Since he couldn't think of anywhere that might admit him in nice, polite Wellington, Makalio decided we should drive over to his home town of Porirua, about twenty miles up the coast.

The Odd Couple, we hardly spoke a word the entire way. According to its official website, Porirua is 'nestled in a stunning harbour setting just 20 minutes north of New Zealand's capital, Wellington'. In fact, it wasn't bad – a small good-looking seaside town stretched lazily across a series of sparkling blue bays. Very New Zealand. We finished up in Makalio's camper van on the beach. Our assistant producer for the programme was Jarrod Gilbert, lecturer in sociology at Canterbury University. An expert on New Zealand's gangs, Gilbert had been my original point of contact with the Mongrel Mob. He decided to join us for a couple of tinnies – nothing like a bit of field work. I asked Gilbert how many gangsters there were in New Zealand. He said that in a population of just over four million, there were no fewer than seventy major gangs with an estimated 4,000 full-time members. No one knows exactly how many of them are in the Mongrel Mob – no one's counting – but with a presence or chapter in most of the country's towns and cities they are by far the biggest gang. There are also quite a few Hell's Angels-style motorcycle gangs, Gilbert told me, among them Satan's Slaves, Highway 61 and the Bandidos. In fact, New Zealand had the first Hell's Angels chapter formed outside the United States – definitely not an answer I'd have got right in a pub quiz.

We sat down and had a beer. After we had drunk ourselves to a complete standstill – or at least I had – I fell asleep. A few hours later I woke up. I couldn't remember a word of what we had been talking about but it was morning and Makalio was prodding me awake with a fresh can of beer. There was no sign of Gilbert. I took the beer. Even though I felt like I'd been embalmed during the night by a team of incompetent morticians, I knew if I didn't drink the can Makalio was holding out then all bets would be off. Leaning back and thinking of the series, I took a swig. Hair of the mongrel.

As we drank, we talked about this and that. I asked Makalio about his 'mask' – the facial tattoos that branded him a gang member. He said, 'To me, it's my belief. I can't run away, it's there for ever. Whatever town I drive to and whatever I do, people know that I represent the Mongrel Mob.'

'Isn't it like giving away your life?' I asked.

He tilted his head. 'It's an identity. And there's no turning back.' Descended from a line of Samoan chiefs, Makalio didn't just wear the Mongrel gang mask on his face and neck, he had ritual Pacific island tribal tattoos all over his lower body. For these ritual markings, the powdered charcoal, ink and spit mixture is hammered into the flesh with a wooden mallet and an ancient toothed whalebone comb. The pain involved is intense; the tattoos invariably go septic and then have to be lanced with a fine bone needle to remove the pus. The few men who undergo it usually have the tattooing spread over a period of six months, with intervals in between for healing. Makalio had the lot done in three days.

I'm still not entirely sure why this happened, but on some level Makalio and I began to connect on that second day. He agreed to tell me about the Mongrel Mob, beginning with a look around his home town. As we drove through the stunningly beautiful scenery, where you expect Bilbo and Frodo Baggins to pop up at any minute, Makalio said that while outsiders like me might think the country revolves around dairy farming, sheep and *The Lord of the Rings*, the Mongrel Mob despises all that, always has done and always will.

As luck would have it, there was a music festival in Porirua later that day, so we went along to take a look. There were a few hundred people in the park enjoying the sounds and the warm summer sunshine. An over-whelmingly Maori event, an alternative New Zealand flag flew over the marquees. A lot of Maoris believe the *pakeha* – the white European immigrants – should get out and leave New Zealand to them.

What surprised me was the way the two or three dozen Mongrel Mob gangsters present mingled freely with the crowds, as if they were an accepted part of everyday life. Like Makalio, the other members were very visible thanks to their facial tattoos and their black and red gang colours, and the fuck-off factor in their appearance was well up to his own high standards. Yet the locals, at any rate, didn't seem to shun the Mob. The kids especially kept coming up and sneaking looks at them or hanging around and watching from a safe distance. Maybe this was part of a recruiting drive. As if to confirm this, when I asked him how he had got started in the gang Makalio said, 'When I was a little kid at primary, there were these two, big ugly mother-fuckers who used to walk around Porirua and they were the meanest and ugliest fucking things on the face of the earth. And I just thought, That's me, man. I wanted to be like that. And I've never looked back since.'

Makalio paused a lot as he spoke, using 'fuck' as a stepping stone to the next word. I noticed that the Mongrel Mob was the only gang at the event. When I commented on this Makalio said, 'There were about eleven gangs in Porirua at one time, but as you see today there is only one gang here. It's the only place in the whole of New Zealand no other gang will come to.'

'Why is that?'

'Because we run it. We cleaned it up.'

'If there were other gangsters here there would be trouble?'

'Hell yeah. But no other gang would come here.'

'What would happen to them?'

Makalio shrugged. 'We both know what would happen.'

What would happen is bad. One notorious gang fight took place in Cathedral Square, Christchurch. I knew this because as part of my research I had seen the graphic video shot by a man in the crowd at the time. When I went to see him a couple of days later, Senior Constable Gary Tibbotts of the Christchurch police told me what he saw that day:

There were probably a thousand people round the square. It was lunchtime. People were sitting down and enjoying the sunshine and the music. Then suddenly, out of nowhere, a fight erupted between two gangs: the Christchurch Mongrel Mob and the Black Power. It was a planned attack. Two or three members of the Mongrel Mob were surrounded by about a dozen Black Power members. The leader of the Black Power gang signalled the start of the attack by holding his two fingers above his head and then bringing them down. Out came knives, lead pipes, chains . . . One of the Mongrel Mob got stabbed with a knife. Another had a bag. He took out an axe. His mate picked up the axe, grabbed one of the opposing gang members and struck him a blow just behind the neck. The axe went through his jacket, two thicknesses, through his jersey and a T-shirt, and just nicked the side of his neck. Miraculously, he escaped fatal injuries.

Exploding in the middle of an arts festival, the fighting was so brazen that many people in the crowd took it for some kind of street theatre. In fact, it was only too real and resulted in several serious injuries. But as my next interviewee, Dave Haslett, formerly of the Christchurch police criminal investigation branch, pointed out, the gangs didn't care. 'What surprised me was how the gangsters didn't seem to mind how many people had been watching.'

'They don't really care? An axe in broad daylight in front of a thousand people?'

'They don't have the same fear that we would have of witnesses seeing something or taking car numbers,' Haslett said. 'Spontaneous violence takes over, and that person will end up getting a kicking or a stomping, or could well end up being stabbed or beaten to death in front of other witnesses.'

To make absolutely sure they know who to attack

when they fight, each Mongrel Mob chapter or regional gang sports a different style of cartoon bulldog on its red and black reggies. Black Power wear black and blue, especially when they go to war, and their badge is a vertical clenched fist.

Since the battle of Wairoa courthouse, the Mongrel Mob has been banned from the town's hotels and bars; its original town-centre clubhouse has been closed down, and the gang exiled to a disused factory on the outskirts. With Makalio riding shotgun, I went along to see it. There were about a dozen gang members in the pad as they call it, and I walked with Dennis across the room to meet them. They called out 'Sieg, bro!' to us. The Mongrel Mob use the Nazi salute all the time to meet and greet, as in, 'She's a good-looking bird – Sieg!'

Most of them were middle aged. A bearded older Mobster told me, 'They have sort of forced us to live the lifestyle we live. But we don't want to go by their system. It is failing already.'

A second man – in shades, full tattoo facial mask and Nazi helmet who looked as if he had just stepped off the set of a film about zombie SS storm troopers – added, 'They forced it on us. Forced control.'

His much younger neighbour said, 'We have tried to change. Tried to keep out of jail, get a few of our members into jobs and that. But . . .' He shrugged.

To get it straight from the horse's mouth, I asked the Wairoa Mob about all the Nazi symbols, language and kit. The older man explained: it was a kind of two fingers to polite, white New Zealand. 'Pissing society off, you know. They don't want to see that, but here we are and no one's going to change it. The country hated Nazism – there was a Maori battalion and everything – so Hitler's sayings . . . symbols – we picked that up and use it to piss society off.'

Makalio agreed: 'I mean, even the abuse of putting a German helmet on a British bulldog, that's an insult. And anything to do with insults, we would wear it.'

At this, the chapter members all shouted, 'Sieg!'

'You still do all that now?'

'We show respect to people that we know that deserve our respect. Otherwise, we don't want to know you. Get out of our road.'

Until then I hadn't realized the Mongrels had picked on the bulldog because it was a wartime symbol of British and Commonwealth defiance. This is a country where many people's parents and grandparents fought and died fighting the Nazis. The Mongrels act as if the Nazis would have been a good alternative, but if Hitler had won and arrived on these shores, I doubt very much whether the gang would have ended up being his best mates.

How did a heavy-duty gang like the Mongrel Mob come to have a presence in most of New Zealand's towns and cities, and hate its society so much? Originally a white gang but now mainly Maori, the Mongrel Mob was formed in Hastings and nearby Napier back in 1968 by kids who said they had been abused in the country's childcare system. Alienated by what they claimed to have suffered at the hands of their supposed carers, the kids formed the Mongrel Mob as a way of striking back, not just at the people they felt had ruined their childhood but at the country as a whole. Forty years down the track, the Mongrel Mob are still exacting their own unique form of revenge although not everyone in the gang knows exactly why and how the Mob got started.

Makalio had introduced me to the real love of his life – always excepting his wife Liz and his kids – a 1964 V8 Ford Galaxie convertible. The key thing about this vehicle for a member of the Mongrel Mob, he told me, was its V8 engine. Classic Fords with V8 engines – the bigger and more powerful the better – are to Mongrel Mobsters what the Harley-Davidson motorcycle is to the Hell's Angels. Some 'Mongies' as they call themselves even have V8 tattooed on their necks. With the Galaxie's hood down we set off across North Island, through Palmerston North, skirting the foothills of the Ruahine Range. I wanted to take a look at Napier and nearby Hastings to see for myself where the Mob got started. I especially wanted to meet one of its few surviving white members, a man named Gary Gerbies. If he had Dennis Makalio's respect, then in Mongrel Mob terms Gerbies had to be something special.

Steering the red Galaxie through a series of sweeping

S-bends in his leisurely style as we made our way north, Makalio told me what had happened when he was starting out in the gang and looking to make his name. He was in a Mongrel clubhouse one day when two local police officers walked in without permission. Just about everyone in New Zealand – and especially the police – knows the Mongrel Mob take extreme exception to uninvited callers. To make things worse, the gang was in the middle of a chapter meeting. The police were asking for trouble, and they got it. 'These two pigs walked in like fucking Starsky and Hutch swinging their batons. I had no commitments. I just fucking went behind them and I shut the door and turned the lights out.' He paused as the memory came back to him and then said, 'Yeah, they fucking got it.'

'How long did you hold them for?'

He made a dismissive gesture. 'Oh, maybe for fifteen minutes.'

'But you were done for torture, weren't you?'

'Torture?' He snorted. 'You know, I was burning them, every fucking thing. I got a lag [prison term] for it, that's why I can talk about it. I got found guilty. Other Mongrels got found guilty just from fucking watching. I'm not ashamed for saying that. They have a problem with the Mongrel Mob – they want us to close up. I'm not going to fucking close up. I'm proud of being a Mongie; I'm proud of talking about the Mongrel Mob.' He shook his head. 'I don't talk about other people. I only talk about me.'

I couldn't help liking this guy, even though he had tortured two policemen. In the process he had taken a step up the Mongrel Mob ladder. He said some of the Mongrels were upset by his decision to talk to me, but Makalio was convinced the Mob should be known much more widely – even globally – for who and what they are. He wasn't just proud of the gang; he was proud of its ideals, which he said came down to three principles: honour, loyalty and respect.

The next morning I had my meeting with Gary Gerbies. Now in his sixties and no longer active in the gang, Gerbies was one of the hardest men I have ever met: not quite as tall as I am but broader, with huge Popeye forearms and ham-sized fists. He had a lumpy broken boxer's face and had lost most of his teeth fighting. I met Gerbies in the living room of his Napier home, and he wasted no time before telling me how he had come by his anger: 'We despised the system because of the treatment we got as social-welfare kids, man. The abuse you got from people who were supposed to be your helpers was bred into us as thirteen-year-old kids. Supposed to be our helpers? They shit on us, man.'

'So you shit back?'

'We shit back and we made them stand up and take notice. We formed a gang, and we took the Nazi swastika as a symbol of rebellion.'

He told me how the Mongrel Mob came by its name. A Hastings District Court judge passing sentence on a group of Mongies had said, 'You are nothing but a pack of mongrels.'

'If you want to call us mongrels and dogs,' Gerbies retorted, 'we'll be it.' The name stuck.

I asked him, 'What does the gang stand for? What does it mean to you?'

He thought for a moment. 'It means a bunch of guys that are friends regardless of what you've been through, where you've been. You've had hard times with each other, you've had good times with each other, but a friend's a friend.'

Gerbies told me how he used to take 'highballs', cocktails of hard drugs, in his heyday. 'We did things to shock people in those days,' he said. As an example he told me a story about a foreign backpacker who had hooked up with one of his best mates. Drinking with them one evening in a Napier bar, Gerbies said the woman started making fun of his friend, Dougie. She made one mocking remark too many. This is what Gerbies and his friend did about it: 'She was sitting on a bar stool. Dougie grabbed her by one leg and ankle and I grabbed her by the other one.' Gerbies stood to demonstrate, raising his arms high above his head. 'We just hoisted her up in the air. Her dress fell down around her head and we tipped her up on the bar. I ripped her fucking pants off with my teeth.'

Seeing my reaction, he lowered his arms and smiled. 'Like I said, we did things to shock people. She had a period. In them days I was crazy, I'd do anything. So I ripped her pants off and I pulled her tampon out of her with my teeth.' He drew a sharp, hissing breath: he was back there in the bar that day, reliving the scene. 'I was slapping it around my face and Dougie was licking all the blood off my face. We were pretty rough people. It was mind-blowing shit.' He laughed, rubbed his bald head and then looked back up at me. 'And then we ate it.'

It certainly was mind-blowing shit. 'You both ate the tampon. And what happened next?'

'A couple of people had a thing about it and moaned so I knocked them down, bashed them up, gave them a hiding. I made love to her on the bar, screwing her in front of everybody.'

'How was she about that?'

He shook his head. 'She enjoyed it.'

'Did she go away after that, or did she hang around?'

'Oh no, she loved it. She was in love with me then. In those days I felt that a lot of women were into aggressive, hard men.'

Right.

I wasn't the only person who found Gerbies hard: when he was young people used to come from miles around to the Napier pubs where Gerbies worked as a bouncer to see if they could beat him in a fistfight. But this was someone who had been fighting since he could walk in a series of orphanages and care homes. Seen for years as one of the hardest men in New Zealand, no one ever succeeded in putting Gerbies down. He told me that he had been put away for murder a couple of times, and even in prison had managed to kill someone, if only by accident. Horsing around with a friend in the prison gymnasium, Gerbies gave his mate what he described as a 'playful tap'. The man fell back, hit the weights bench on the way down and snapped his neck. Some playful taps are harder than others.

Despite all the horrible things he might have done in his life, Gerbies was fascinating. A part of me liked him. He told me a funny story about his reggies. While he was in prison for murder he bought some new jeans to make into reggies and hung them over the grille where the inmates emptied their buckets when they slopped out. Going for the world-record smelliest reggies, Gerbies left the jeans there for several years. On his release from prison he took them home. His mother promptly threw them out. Gerbies never spoke to her again.

Leaving Gerbies with the bar scene he had told me about ringing in my head, I went to see Makalio again. I found it hard to believe that any woman, even back in the late 1970s, would have enjoyed what had happened that day. I wanted his take on it. Makalio told me that when it comes to the Mongrel Mob, some women are like groupies round a rock star: 'They love a dog.'

'You told me you've got fan clubs.'

'We've got fan clubs.'

'Explain a fan club to me?' He shook his head and took a long drag of the cigarette he had going. 'A fan club is just a whole load of bitches that look after a soldier – look after a brother without him getting into any fucking shit.'

'They protect them? They fuck them?' Makalio nodded. 'Fucking right.'

Since it was nearby and Makalio had set it up for me, I went over to see the Mongrel Mob Hastings chapter pad. After hearing about what had happened to the two policemen Makalio attacked in Porirua, I made sure the invitation was rock solid. A big old shed of wood and corrugated iron painted in Mongrel red, the pad was at the end of a track off a quiet street. Inside, it was a gloomy barn of a place with a bar at the back and a pool table in front of that. MIGHTY MONGREL MOB was painted in huge white letters behind the bar. There were six or seven gang members sitting around a table covered in a blood-red cloth waiting for me. It looked as if they had been in the place drinking all night. A girl of about three years old dressed in a Mongrel red tracksuit was playing with the pool balls. She was the daughter of one of the gang. Three of the mobsters were wearing Nazi helmets. Most had full tattoo masks. One Mobster's face didn't really have any tattooed words or designs, it was just solid ink. He wore sunglasses, and his lips quivered convulsively as if from the effects of crystal methamphetamine abuse.

The clubhouse walls were covered in gang regalia – cartoon bulldogs everywhere, including the Hastings chapter's own emblem. They told me the Mob has adopted – or adapted – some things from the US Hell's Angels gangs. Most chapters have a president and a sergeant-at-arms. The sergeant-at-arms acts as the chapter's enforcer when any of its members step out of line. Before they are admitted, anyone who wants to join the Mongrel Mob has to serve time as a 'prospect' – hanging around doing bad stuff with patched men. Sometimes, they told me, guys spend years as prospects before the Mob will let them join.

At initiation into the Mob, many chapters make the prospect fight selected gang members. If he gives a good enough account of himself, he's in, and moves on to the next stage: masking and patching. A new man can choose how much he wants done, but the tattoos on his face are in almost every case so uncompromising they lock him into the Mongrel Mob for life. This helps keep up Mob numbers, ensures its survival and more or less guarantees none of its members will grass on the gang.

The Hastings Mongrels launched into a drunken gang ballad that began, 'We are the members of the Mongrel Mob / We drink all night and we fuck like dogs / We put women on the block / They love the satisfaction of a Mongrel's cock / Sieg heil, Sieg heil, Sieg heil!' They broke off to give me the Mob salute and bark. To salute they made an M shape with their hands and raised them over their heads. They were singing about the fact that if a woman other than a wife or girlfriend of a Mob member comes into one of the chapter pads uninvited, then just like the New Zealand police she does it at her own risk. But the Mongrel Mob doesn't torture and beat women. Instead, they put her on the 'block'. The block might be the pool table the little girl in the background was playing on, or it can be an actual block of wood or a box the mobsters keep handy for uninvited – or for that matter invited – female callers. When I asked him about this, Makalio insisted it was not rape: 'A chick knows what the story is if she's going to come knocking on the door. She knows she's only in there to feed us. She has to assume the fucking position.'

At the end of the week I had a day off to chill out. When I met up with Makalio again, he was washing down Mongrel Mob headstones in a Porirua cemetery. For him, the graves of fallen gang members are places of pilgrimage. Most of the headstones were black marble with an inset Mongrel Mob patch. There were also presents left for the dead, and their favourite possessions. The Mongrels die in all kinds of ways – in car accidents, shootings and stabbings, drug overdoses – but Lester Epps, the gangster whose grave Makalio had come to tend, had been killed by a rugby league team. 'It took the whole rugby team to kill this fellow. He was asleep outside the pad; he'd just finished coming back from the pub that night and he'd given quite a few of them a good crack.'

'He'd been to the pub, beaten a few of these rugby league guys up?'

'Yeah. They came round, and they got him at about five, six o'clock in the morning.' Epps was beaten so badly he died of his injuries in hospital three days later. The members of the rugby team involved in the assault each got eighteen months in prison. Epps was twenty-six when he died.

Sometimes, when a well-respected gang member dies the Mobsters commandeer the corpse, prop it up in the dead man's car, stick a cigarette in his mouth and a beer in his hand, and take him out for a final party. The grieving family are not always too happy about a bunch of Mongies turning up and grabbing their loved one's corpse. When they finally bury him, the Mongrels sometimes have the dead man's engine block sandblasted, rustproofed and the air filter patched with the chapter insignia and use that as a grave marker.

Makalio said he looked after gang graves that were left untended because he believed in the Mongrel Mob, in its traditions and core code of honour, loyalty and respect. But the problem for him and older gang members like him was the erosion of this code. Old-timers don't believe the new generation is upholding the true Mongrel gang spirit. 'Drugs,' Makalio said tightly, 'are ruining it.'

He said that whereas in the past the Mongrel Mob had banded together and taken on the world, for the younger guys now it was all about money and drugs:

more and more crystal methamphetamine was coming into New Zealand from Asia, and at the same time more of it was also being 'cooked' in the country. Like their customers, many Mongrel Mob members were getting addicted to the drug, which in its pure form is known locally as 'P'. Given the chance of making big money many of the older mobsters, too, were joining the drugs trade, dealing marijuana and manufacturing and supplying P to the growing market.

Makalio said, 'A gang member in the old days might try a little bit of LSD or whatever was around, pot and that. But at the end of the day that shit would slow you down. The difference is, back then there was nothing wrong with having a buzz. But if you were caught out to be a fucking junkie you'd get kicked out or given a fucking good hiding. Today, it's sad, but I think they've just forgotten that. I talk about how I love the Mob – I'll never leave and all that – but there's one thing that would most probably make me leave the Mob – if I see it all turning to junkies.'

Makalio saw that drugs risked undermining the gang from within. Speaking to me over the grave of another Mob friend who had taken his own life he said, 'A lot of people have forgotten our bros that have passed away. They're forgetting everything. I just want to bring that tightness back, that brotherhood.' It was like listening to the last man of his tribe.

On leaving the cemetery where Epps and other Mongrel Mobsters were buried, I forgot to rinse my hands in the bowl of water usually placed at the entrance to a New Zealand graveyard, particularly Maori sites. The idea is to wash away the spirits of the dead. I don't believe in ghosts, but that night I had the worst nightmares of my life. I woke up in a cold sweat, staring at the walls and wondering where I was. Now, any time I visit a burial place, I give my hands a thorough wash on the way out.

As a break from filming during my second week in New Zealand, Makalio took me to a rugby league match between North Island and South Island Mongrel Mobsters. It was one of the most violent games of rugby I have ever seen: there didn't seem to be any rules and the referee didn't seem to mind when someone gouged an opponent's eye or landed a punch. The violence threatened to become personal when one of the gang came up and told me in no uncertain terms I wasn't wanted.

While we were watching the match, another Mobster told me about a Mongrel who had been asked to act as a paid bouncer at a middle-class family wedding. He said he couldn't name the man, and once I had heard the story I could understand why. Everything was going fine at the feast until the bouncer had one drink too many and tried to grope a couple of female guests. When he learned what had happened, the bridegroom got the rest of the men together and threw the Mobster out on his ear.

Some months later the Mongrel in question was out driving with a female friend when he spotted the bridegroom cycling along the road up ahead. He felt he had been humiliated. It stuck in his craw. Now, he decided, it was payback time. He floored the accelerator, raced up behind the bloke and rammed into him. By some fluke the bridegroom's head came clean off his shoulders, smashed in through the car windscreen and ended up on the passenger's lap. The man's jaw was still working up and down. Shocked to the marrow, the woman started screaming hysterically. The Mongrel told her to shut up and calm down. When she kept on screaming he punched her into unconsciousness, threw the victim's head out of the window and drove on.

Just in case I was getting too close to the Mongrel Mob and starting to believe they were not all that bad, Jarrod Gilbert took me to the site of an infamous rape and murder that had happened outside Napier in 1989. The victim, a pretty sixteen-year-old schoolgirl named Colleen Burrows, had told her mother, Ida Hawkins, she was just popping into town with some other members of the family to get some food. It was a fifteen-minute drive from where they lived. Instead of returning with the takeaway, Burrows and the others ended up in a bar drinking with a couple of Mongrel Mobsters who took Burrows on to a party and later, after more drinks, propositioned her. Her mother told me what happened next: 'They'd taken her down the

riverbank for sex. She never gave in to their demands.'
Mrs Hawkins began to cry as she remembered what
had been done to her daughter. 'They booted her
brutally with their steel-capped boots. Kicked her body.
And left her lying there.'

Jeff Gunn, the now retired police officer who investigated the murder, took up the story: 'They drove off
in the vehicle. As they were driving off they noticed
she was still moving. They turned the vehicle around
some distance from her at that stage, and then drove
back towards her.'

Ida Hawkins again: 'They ran her over, I don't know
how many times. And left her lying there.' The injuries
to the body were so bad the police were only able to
identify it because of its distinctive tattoos.

The two men had stripped Burrows, beaten her,
raped her, beaten her again and then run her over.
Arrested, T. K. Sullivan and Samuel Tahai eventually
confessed and got life in prison. Gunn says, 'When he
[Tahai] finally did admit to his involvement he could
have been admitting to stealing a car or doing a burglary.
No remorse at all, just a shrug of the shoulders.'

On the day I went to visit the dead girl's grave,
it was pouring with rain. Whatever Tahai felt or did
not feel, watching Ida Hawkins weep for her daughter
certainly got to me.

When he found out I was going to include the story
in the programme, Makalio got upset, insisting the gang
doesn't rape any more. But it happened and is far from

being the only time Mongrel Mobsters have attacked and raped. Another example of the Mob at its worst, and one that set virtually the whole of New Zealand against the gang, took place in Ambery Park, Auckland, in December 1986. Wisely or not, the city authorities had allowed the Mob to gather in the park for a 'convention', otherwise known as a massive drink-up. The Mobsters duly met and drank, and then some of them spotted a woman walking her dog along a street bordering the venue. Grabbing her right off the pavement in broad daylight, they took her to a secluded corner of the park and gang-raped her. Others joined in, raping the victim repeatedly in an attack that lasted for several hours. When she at last managed to escape and hid behind a stage, the woman made the mistake of asking another Mongrel if he would help her get away. Promising to do so, the man instead led her back to the pack. Many of them raped her again.

While some countries segregate warring gangs in prison, in New Zealand the policy is to put the Mongrel Mob and Black Power together on the same wing. The idea – call it hope – is that this will force them to get along. Does it work? Bryan Christy, site manager at Auckland prison, says it does. What may not work so well, as far as I could make out from talking to gang members, is putting them in prison at all. Some told me they looked on their time behind bars as a kind of rest: a chance to get free of drugs, down some square meals and get into better physical shape. They also claim to run the prisons. When I put this to Christy, he said,

I don't believe they run the prison. We monitor their activities and see how things go. If it starts looking like the Mongrel Mob is starting to tool themselves up we'll close the place down and do a pretty thorough search. If there's a need to separate individuals we will do that. Having a big war or a scrap doesn't faze these guys: it's just part of their lifestyle. They hate each other with a vengeance, sure, and there have been occasions where we've had brothers in different gangs in this place and they have to fight against each other. That is a sad thing. A lot of people can't understand it, but that's the way they are, that's how strong the code is.

Mongrel Mobsters also claim that prison is where they recruit most of their new gang members and that for every two Mongrels sent to prison another two leave and take their place. I watched them play 'crash' rugby in the prison gym with no thought for their personal safety. Just as in life outside, they were prepared to risk anything to win.

The methamphetamine problem in New Zealand is now considered so serious that no individual is allowed more than seven prescriptions a year for drugs that contain pseudoephedrine, the main constituent of P. Used mainly in cold and flu remedies, pseudoephedrine is cooked out of the tablets, often in home labs, turned into crystal meth and then sold at a gigantic mark-up. As addictive as crack cocaine – some users say more so, in that the hit lasts much longer – crystal meth drives its users to commit almost any crime to feed their need. It can also dissolve their facial bones and kill them. After being in the country for a couple of weeks I could see that P is going to be a massive problem for everyone in New Zealand over the coming years, including the country's various gangs. Drugs tend to split gangs, most often when members start to quarrel about money.

In October 2004 Detective Sergeant Ross Tarawhiti of the Christchurch police launched a massive fifteen-month investigation into the activities of the Christchurch Mongrel Mob, codenamed Operation Crusade because the Mongrels' pad was situated next door to the Crusaders rugby club ground. Maintaining round-the-clock surveillance on the gang, officers covertly taped hundreds of hours of telephone conversations between its members. Said Tarawhiti, 'The operation began as a result of tensions within the Mongrel Mob. There were leadership problems – they were fighting among themselves. The police were being called to gang members' addresses where other gang members were breaking and smashing their way in using baseball bats and stabbing their own guys. The whole gang was starting to fall apart.'

'They were quite brazen about the way they were

selling their drugs. They weren't exactly hiding it, were they?' I said.

Tarawhiti shook his head. 'They don't care. They just go out there and do the business.' The police discovered Mongrel Mobsters worked a roster, with drug peddling the most important part of their duties. But according to Tarawhiti, it was here things went wrong for the gang: 'The funny thing about the whole operation was, they were in the business of selling and they were actually ripping each other off. Quite a few of the members were using quite a bit of the product themselves. And then telling other people that for one reason or another the money had gone.' Raids on gang premises turned up drugs, ammunition and further evidence of dealing. The evidence gathered led to New Zealand's biggest ever drugs trial. Fifteen Mongrel Mobsters were convicted on charges that included dealing methamphetamine and cannabis, and possessing guns and ammunition. At a stroke, the police had taken out the entire leadership of the Mongrel Mob's Christchurch chapter. For good measure, they bulldozed flat the gang's fortified headquarters at 460 Wilson's Rd.

Commenting on the bigger drugs picture in New Zealand since then, Tarawhiti said, 'Methamphetamine is bad news as far as the police are concerned because it alters people's behaviour, makes them violent. It's causing a lot of problems within the gang too, a lot of their members are dropping dead because of it.'

Whether or not the many convictions will help rid

Christchurch of the Mongrel Mob in the longer term remains to be seen. But it certainly slows them down.

Leaving New Zealand was and remains one of the strangest – and most moving – experiences of my life. After I'd been drinking with Makalio and Gilbert all night, Liz, Makalio's wife, drove us to Napier airport, where I was scheduled to board a small, twin-prop aircraft bound for Auckland on the first leg of the journey home. With several crates to help us on our way, we necked tinnies of Steinlager at a steady rate. Napier is a small airfield. As we arrived, I looked up to see a party of middle-aged white ladies dressed in blue blazers and white pleated skirts waiting to board the same flight – a local ladies' bowls team off to play the Auckland opposition.

Dennis wasn't content with just dropping me off; he wanted to see me onto the plane. I went to shake his hand, but he grabbed me, pulled me towards him and did the South Sea Island nose rub. We hugged. In the short time we had spent together we had become good friends. It may be hard for people reading this to understand, but we both had tears in our eyes. I turned and walked away to board the plane. He put his head back and 'barked me out' in true Mongrel Mob style – a series of harsh guttural barks cut with long, baying howls. The ladies around me in the queue boarding the plane tutted and shushed and shot disapproving looks, but in that moment I felt more connection with the

Mongrel Mob than I ever would with any bowls team. On the steps of the plane I turned, lifted my arm and waved a final salute to Dennis Makalio.

To this day he remains a friend.

3. El Salvador

I knew very little about El Salvador before setting foot in the place. But the second the crew and I cleared customs one thing jumped right out at me: the country is awash with guns. The police have them, and there were plenty of officers in and around the airport; the armed forces were out on the streets – there was a roadblock on the main highway into the capital, San Salvador; and if what little I had heard about El Salvador was true, the gangsters have even more of them.

Taking in all the weapons on display I started to get an uneasy feeling, the kind you get before something really bad happens. Tom Gibb, the BBC's South America correspondent, our local translator and first point of contact with the gangs, didn't lessen my apprehension by pointing out that in a country the size and population of Wales there are at least a dozen murders a day. The vast majority are carried out by El Salvador's two deadly rival gangs, Mara Salvatrucha 13 (MS13, also known as the El Salvador Gang) and 18 Street, known to its enemies as the 'foreigners' on account of its ethnic Mexican origins.

Statistically the most violent and aggressive gangs on the planet, MS13 and 18 Street operate mainly in the place where we were now headed – the capital city, San Salvador – but before we even got there El Salvador lived up to its murderous reputation. Lying in the dirt at the side of the road was the body of a man. We slowed, and then crawled to a stop. I got out to take a look with Andy Thomson and our director. Dressed in blue jeans and a red T-shirt, the dead man lay sprawled where he had fallen. There was blood and bits of brain on the grey-brown mud around what was left of his head. The crime scene was taped off with orange traffic cones and yellow and black DO NOT CROSS police tape. The rest of the traffic roared by at our backs without stopping. A bus rolled up and started to let off passengers. I hadn't realized it until then, but we were at a bus stop. I asked one of the officers what had happened. 'This man was a bus conductor. He was twenty years old. He has been executed with a single shot to the head. It happened this morning, in front of all the people on the bus.' I stared down at the body. The officer added, 'They shot the driver also, but we have already taken his body away. He too was killed by a single shot to the head.'

'Why would anybody want to kill a bus crew?' I asked.

The policeman shrugged. 'The gangs make the bus operators pay money to cross their *clica* – their turf. If they refuse . . .' He left the sentence unfinished. But the price of refusing the gangsters' extortion was only too plain. This was a piece of human gang graffiti, a warning to others who might think of refusing to pay. We left the young bus conductor lying with the remains of the takeaway he had been eating at the moment of his death strewn around him.

Following this first-hand experience of cold-blooded murder, the morgue seemed like a good place to start finding out more about the country's gangs. San Salvador's city morgue is a large tin and concrete warehouse lined with freezer cabinets. It stands next to a couple of other large tin and concrete blocks that turned out to be the central criminal court and beyond that the police station. As we drove up to the entrance, a grieving family was loading the body of a young teenager into the back of a pickup. His mother, father and brothers had brought along their own coffin in which to bury him. The victim of an unexplained gang stabbing, the boy had been just seventeen years old when he died.

We walked into the courthouse. All around us there were rows of handcuffed youths, most heavily tattooed on the face and body with their respective gang insignia. Some covered their heads with their shirts when they saw the camera, but most gave us gang recognition hand signs, smiling proudly while they did it. When I remarked on the number of kids awaiting trial, Gibb said, 'This is a very, very violent country. I really hoped at the end of the civil war there would be peace, but in fact the violence has carried on at almost the same rate. It was a war in which 2 per cent of the population was

Street kids in Borel

A Borel street kid testing the poor quality foundations of a local shack

What it's all about

Everywhere you go, the Comando Vermelho gang has marked its territory

Third command TC high on ecstasy

The Borel CV head honcho with his best friend on his lap

Enough guns to start a small war

A battery farm for humans – 150 prisoners held in cells meant for 15

Clapping and chanting to the evangelical Christians' music

Me and Dennis with his V8

Social event for Mongrel Mobsters in Porirua

Hastings mobster

Me and the guys in
Wairoa

Dennis and me

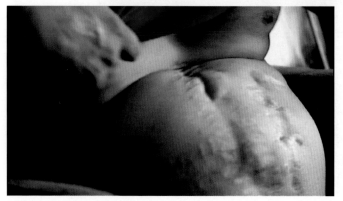

Mahi Kamona's patched-up stomach after nearly being disembowelled

Small Psychopaths'
memorial in
Delgado, El
Salvador

Inmates in Ciudad Barrios

Hugo is the one in the T-shirt, and his scary enforcer is on the far left. All these guys were tough, but the enforcer was in a league of his own.

Removing make-up to show off tattoos

Chucho visiting his wife, Ingrid, in Susaltepeque prison and meeting his baby daughter for the first time

killed – in British terms that would be a million people. And the legacy of that violence has continued. There's a war going on between the two main gangs, and there are daily killings.' He nodded at the court building. 'That's really the two ways out for an awful lot of gang members. They're either brought here and then go on to jail' – he switched his gaze to the morgue – 'or they are brought there dead.'

Just then a police SWAT team brought in a suspect. In his early twenties, the guy had an evil look on him – a flat cold steady-eyed stare that warned you to steer clear. Whatever he had done it had to have been bad – the SWAT men stood close and never once took their eyes off him. In standard black fire-retardant coveralls and boots, they were armed with M16s, M4s, sub-machine guns, knives, machetes, semi-automatic pistols and even in the stifling heat wore black balaclavas to protect their identities. The captain in charge told me this is because many officers live in the *clicas* cheek by jowl with the gangsters they fight. He said the suspect was a leading 18 Street gang member.

The prisoner, in a bright scarlet silk shirt, began to get cocky and really pleased with himself when this foreigner showed interest in him. Grinning, he refused to answer any of my questions except to claim he did not understand why he had been arrested. Next day, I found out the reason he might have been so reluctant to talk: under banner headlines that screamed 'Leader of the Child Killers!' the same suspect's name and face were all over the front pages of El Salvador's rabid tabloid newspapers. He was accused of murdering two small children to stop the family testifying against another 18 Street gangster about to go on trial for a separate crime.

The next day I went to meet a MS13 sub-gang Tom Gibb had managed to make contact with in one of the *clicas*, the gang neighbourhoods I kept hearing about. (The word *clica* is used to refer both to the neighbourhood and the sub-gangs themselves.) The gangsters said they might be prepared to talk to us.

When we got to the *clica* in question, we spotted five guys outside a collection of tumbledown shacks built on a hillside a few hundred metres up a disused overgrown railway line. The only access to the *clica* was via a narrow rickety railway bridge, which helped keep the police and the wrong kind of gangster at bay. The housing was close to rock bottom, self-build shacks with running water and electricity stolen from the mains. There was washing hanging everywhere and all around the lush green of encroaching plant life. The gangsters wore jeans and vests or T-shirts or no shirts at all. There was a very strong smell of excrement.

After some staring and glaring as we climbed the narrow steps up towards them, the boys started yelling, 'Mary Jane, Mary Jane!' This didn't strike me as being very friendly. I can be in touch with my metropolitan side, but give me a break, guys. But then Gibb leaned across and told me I shouldn't take it as an insult: Mary Jane was their nickname for the massive marijuana spliffs they were all smoking.

I went forward to make contact. At first, their leader didn't want to admit to being the top man. A fidgety-looking guy named Omar, with restless eyes and a wiry build, his gang name was Chucho. The monicker suited him. Chucho said the gang was called the Small Psychopaths of Delgado City – Delgado City being the name of the San Salvador *clica* where we were now standing. It wasn't much of a city, more a mudslide waiting to happen. The Psychopaths were certainly small. And dark-haired and wiry. But what came across as we stood there was how young they were. They didn't look like a gang of murderers, 'the second biggest threat to America after al-Qaeda', as the FBI put it. They looked like a bunch of scared teenage kids.

Chucho claimed the Small Psychopaths operated a strict 'blood in, blood out' rule. In theory this meant that each and every one of the five men in front of me had killed someone to join the gang. He told me that when he was four years old a gang of 18 Street assassins had shot his father dead. His mother was still alive. His main girlfriend was in prison – as was their baby daughter. The girl was now eight months old but Chucho had never seen her. Still only in his mid-twenties, Chucho had two more daughters by another woman – eight and eleven years old – but he hardly ever dared go and see them. As one of the local 18 Street gang's priority targets, every time he showed his face anywhere near any of his extended family he put them at severe risk. 'They've got my family involved, so my family is scared too.'

Chucho couldn't remember how many times he had been arrested and locked up, it had happened so often. Released the week before we met him after ten months in prison for possession of marijuana, Chucho said he had joined MS13 when he was about fifteen. As we spoke he took deep drags from the spliff smouldering between his long, skinny fingers. The day he was let out of prison last time around, seven 18 Street gunmen came along the railway line looking for him. He ran and hid in the bushes until they had gone. He told us he was scared to leave the house because of the way 18 Street kept on coming. 'Every now and again, they come looking to kill me.' One look in his eyes was enough for me to work out the truth: this was a man who felt guilty – and no wonder. 'They killed my brother – he was deaf and dumb. It was because of me. I'm the one in the gang. He wasn't in it, but that didn't matter to them.'

The heartless killing of Chucho's fifteen-year-old brother is typical of what the gangs in El Salvador get up to every day, fuelling a cycle of homicidal gang-on-gang violence that shows no signs of ending any time soon. Chucho made it clear he wasn't just on the receiving end; he dished it out, too.

The youngest and smallest member of the Small

Psychopaths was a twenty-year-old nicknamed Joker. The *clica*'s chief executioner, according to Chucho, Joker smiled that little bit too much. No doubt he smiled while he was shooting people. He told me he had joined the Small Psychos 'when I was very young – about nine'. At first the other gangsters had nicknamed him *mascota*, mascot. Both Joker's parents were still alive, but they had kicked him out of the house when he joined MS13. Two of his brothers were also in MS13, but in a different *clica*. Joker said that although they all paid MS13 rent for the use of the local *clica* house or *distroya*, he was the only member of the Small Psychopaths who actually lived there – the others kept on moving around, so as not to get tracked down and shot.

Smiling broadly, Joker, who stood about five feet tall in his socks, toked his Mary Jane as if his life depended on it. In between hits on the weed, he said that hanging around the 'hood was pretty much all the Small Psychos did every day. At night they went out hunting 18 Street. As Chucho put it, 'Often they've hurt someone in our family; we can't let them get away with it.' He should know.

I asked, 'If someone from 18 Street came here, what would be your response?'

This made them all laugh. 'If they came we would just kill them.' They all carried handguns hidden in their waistbands. Chucho let me take a look at his Argentine army 9-millimetre. That would make a hole in you all right.

'What is the conflict between the two gangs based on?' I asked.

Chucho made a rectangle with his hands. 'We defend this area because this is where we live. We look after it and we can't let them come and operate here. This is El Salvador and Mara Salvatrucha are in control. We are not going to let any other gang exist here.' They look on 18 Street as a Mexican gang that has come south.

The more we talked, the more I realized that my first impression of these guys had been completely wrong. They weren't just kids; they were very bad news – full-time, professional armed gangsters. In fact, given the record of shooting and murder that gradually unfolded as we talked together over the next few days, the gang name they had chosen was a bit of an understatement.

I had the strong feeling that Chucho was a man living with more than just regret. High on the neighbouring 18 Street hit list, he knew his every waking moment might be his last – or even a sleeping moment, for that matter. The other thing that kept Chucho and the others inside their home *clica* was the fear that the police would rearrest them on sight because of their criminal records and tattoos. As a bit of a change from the usual demonic MS13 gang symbols, Chucho had a full cemetery tattooed on his left arm, with each of the grave names marking one of his dead 'homeboys' or fellow gang members. Out of more than fifty founding members when the Small Psychopaths had been formed back in 1992, the gang had only seven remaining active members. Most had been shot dead. This probably explained the lack of new recruits. Others were in prison and a few had simply vanished without trace.

I asked him about his children. Thinking about the question, Chucho held in the Mary Jane smoke for as long as he could, as if he was in a hold-your-breath competition. Finally, he admitted that he didn't want them to lead the same kind of life as him. But he himself could never leave the gang – he said there was nothing else he could do with his life. Looking round, it was hard to disagree.

The next man in line said his name was Groupie. Harder-looking than Chucho, his face and arms were scarred more than tattooed, although MS13 was inked large on his chest. Groupie too had spent many of his twenty-seven years in prison. Members of 18 Street had murdered his father when he was one year old; then, when he was twelve, they murdered his mother for good measure. In more recent times they had shot and killed his uncle. He lived with his elder sister, who had helped raise him. Groupie had joined the gang to get revenge. You could kind of see his point. A lot less forthcoming than his leader, Groupie complained the police harassed the Small Psychopaths the whole time, and the gang was sick of it. A heavy drinker, he said he was trying to go on the wagon but was finding it extremely difficult.

Miguel, the *clica*'s most recent recruit, had joined the gang only a year and a half before we met him. Despite having reached the ripe old age of twenty-four, Miguel still lived with his mother, a short way down the railway line from Chucho. But the fact that an 18 Street *clica* occupied the turf directly between meant that social visits were a tad risky. Like the others, Miguel had been arrested for *asociación ilícita* (illegal association) and served ten months in prison.

In an effort to stem the tide of criminality that threatens to engulf the country, in 1999 El Salvador brought in a law known as *mano dura*. Loosely translated as 'iron fist', this is the country's equivalent of America's RICO Act. Anyone suspected of criminal association can be arrested without all that bothersome business of collecting hard evidence. They are kept on remand for as long as it takes to establish their guilt or, rarely, innocence. In practice, *mano dura* has meant that hundreds of MS13 and 18 Street gang members have been swept up off the streets and sent to prison for no other reason than having prominent gang tattoos. The unintended consequence? Gangsters now tend to get themselves tattooed from the neck down and the elbow up, leaving no visible outward sign of their affiliation. Miguel's tattoos, for instance, were small and on his arms.

A second outcome has been to drive the gangs that little bit further underground. Some of the gangsters have also started moving upmarket, at least in the way they dress, wearing stuff like tennis clothes so they are harder to spot. They also spend a lot less time out on the streets. However, the worst result of *mano dura* is that now, instead of simply getting 'jumped' or beaten up when they join, some crews make new recruits kill a member of an opposing gang. The idea behind this policy is to lock new members in: once you have murdered someone and the rest of the gang know about it, you are very much less likely to turn grass.

Listening to the way the Small Psychos talked about their 18 Street enemies hammered home the visceral hatred between them. Neither gang acknowledges the other by name – it's always the 'people in the other neighbourhood' or the 'foreigners'. Naming them would only be giving them respect. Imagine being in a permanent state of armed conflict with your next-door neighbours but not about fences, over-loud music or how high your hedges have grown. Your neighbours want to kill you, and they know you want to do the same to them. That's how it is all the time if you are in one of these gangs. The Small Psychopaths told me that if they met a rival gang member anywhere at any time, they had to kill him – that was the code.

They didn't just use semi-automatic pistols: the gang's big chief, Ronaldo, or Blue, who was currently in prison, had blown his right hand off when he fell on a home-made grenade and it exploded. Warming up a bit, Chucho launched into a rant about how the government was the real problem in El Salvador: it used the *clica* gangs both as a convenient scapegoat and as a smokescreen for its own illegal activities. Especially, he insisted, its direct involvement in the cocaine trade. At the time I didn't believe him. Later on I became less sure.

From the gang members I'd seen in detention at the courthouse, MS 13 and 18 Street are exactly alike. They looked the same, they dressed the same, and no doubt they enjoyed themselves the same. I told Chucho, 'They have tattoos the same as you too.'

He shook his head. 'Yes, but they are different tattoos.' The gangs were the same but they killed each other because they had different tattoos? Now, I *really* didn't understand.

Anticipating death on a daily basis, the Small Psychos lived life in the fast lane: every time I saw Joker he had another set of love bites from a different girl. They claimed they both made and dealt in firearms, especially shotguns. Helps keep up the murder rate. Their lives were about drugs, alcohol, murder, sex and music, in any order and frequently several of them at the same time. Shooting at and getting shot by their 18 Street neighbours was an everyday reality. For the Small Psychopaths, death was a way of life.

Gangs need constant supplies of fresh blood or they wither and die. Most gangs feed off the local population, sucking members up in a never-ending cycle of poverty and hatred. In the case of 18 Street's male members, initiation involves getting savagely beaten by a circle of established gang members for eighteen seconds – or for as long as you can endure it. The longer you can take it, the higher your ranking in the gang. For MS13 similar rules apply. It's supposed to be thirteen seconds, but no one is standing there with a stopwatch. When people are hitting you as hard as they can, any seconds at all is a very long time. But the men don't get raped.

The initiation process is so vicious the gangs have a real problem recruiting young women. No surprises there. So here's what some do to keep up the numbers: female gang members pick a young woman from their local neighbourhood. She's usually strong and good looking – that's what the men like, and that's the type of person the gang needs. First, they go to the targeted girl and invite her politely to join the gang. If she refuses, the women surround the girl and invite her to choose between the same violent 'jumping' as the men, which can leave you with missing teeth, broken bones and/or facially scarred for life, and the 'train'.

The train is gang rape. Anyone can get on board and take a ride. If a girl chickens out of the beating and opts for the train, the rape doesn't end there: she has to make herself available to any gangster who wants to use her sexually at any time for as long as she lives. If she tries to resist, then the gang kill her.

To make sure she can never leave the gang the gangsters use a tattoo gun to etch MS13 or 18 STREET across the victim's forehead and cheeks in great big glaring blue-black ink. Once she has the facial tattoos no other man will touch her: she belongs to the gang and can never again lead a normal life.

Squeezed into the south-western corner of the isthmus that connects North and South America, the little rain-forest republic of El Salvador has to be one of the least fortunate, most blighted countries on the face of the planet. It sits on a tectonic fault line that boasts no fewer than six active volcanoes. These trigger regular serious eruptions, earthquakes and tremors. There was a tremor while I was there: feeling the earth move beneath your feet adds a certain spice to the daily round.

In January 2001 an earthquake measuring 7.6 on the Richter scale triggered landslides that killed more than 1,200 people and left roughly 250,000 homeless. One month later a second quake killed at least 250 people and seriously damaged thousands more homes. This tiny country also happens to have the highest population density in Latin America – 245 people per square kilometre. There is also a serious and growing Aids problem. A very bad year, 2001 also saw one of El Salvador's worst ever droughts, which destroyed more than 80 per cent of the crops and gave rise to yet another of the country's periodic famines. As a result of these, most of the country's once rich and diverse wildlife has disappeared into the stomachs of the starving.

Then there is the weather. For most of the time, as

the porter in my hotel helpfully pointed out, there are only two kinds of weather in El Salvador: mud or dust. Thick, heavy and humid, the equatorial heat beats you down. The low grey cloud that seems to clag the sky up most days traps and intensifies the heat, and when it rains, it rains like nowhere else I've ever been. If you have ever stood in a tropical monsoon, then you understand what really heavy rain can be like. El Salvador's downpours pick up a monsoon and run with it, with raindrops that give you a good slap if you are follically challenged like me. When it hits the tin roofs all around it sounds like a war's going on. The effect of all this pounding is that floods and mudslides also figure heavily in the national litany of woe. In addition the country is malarial, and other tropical diseases are widespread. We still haven't mentioned the odd tropical hurricane, like Mitch, which killed more than 200 people in 1998. Funny how they always give these killer cyclones a friendly-sounding name.

As if natural disasters weren't enough, El Salvador's roads are lethal. One of the most dangerous things you can do here is something that would be completely normal in the UK – drive somewhere, especially in the countryside at night. That's when the gangsters come out to play. Heavily armed thugs ambush any likely-looking vehicle at gunpoint and fleece its occupants. The slightest sign of resistance or failure to hand over your valuables gets you shot.

There seems to be no formal driving test, or if there

is you can bypass it with a bribe. Most people drive at breakneck speed without troubling their indicators or rear-view mirrors. As far as I could see, it is considered a sign of weakness to give way to oncoming traffic, and since people drive in the middle of the road where the surface tends to be best, there are quite a few head-on collisions. Carcasses of animals mown down by speeding drivers lie rotting by the side of the road or on it – another reason why there is hardly any exotic wildlife left in El Salvador. It is important to avoid the larger corpses as your car can turn over, making you part of the general carnage.

Then there's the smog. We in the First World might angst about global warming, but I suppose we can afford to. In El Salvador few people seem to care about the environment. In the resulting free-for-all, some of the world's filthiest vehicles chug around cheerfully polluting what's left of the air. One of these – a giant truck – came close to killing us early in the shoot.

We were travelling behind it on day three. The exhaust fumes belching from its tailpipes were so dense that despite staying at what should have been a safe distance, we could hardly see the road in front of us. Without any warning – like brake lights – the truck driver stood on his air brakes. The juggernaut screeched to a halt. Our Land Cruiser kept going – and going. With my right foot flat to the floor on the brake pedal I wished was there, I saw the back of the truck looming up. Scenes from my past life flashed before me. At the last instant, our driver, José, swerved, missing the truck by an inch. At fifty miles an hour, if we had hit the outcome would not have been good. I turned to José and asked why he hadn't stopped sooner. Peering through his bifocals, he croaked, 'I don't see so good in the dark.' I pointed out it was broad daylight.

As if things like this didn't make driving difficult enough, the roads are thick with roadblocks. The police and army in El Salvador must have more of these breeze-block barriers set up at any one time than the rest of the world put together. To make things worse, breeze blocks are quite often hard to see against the tarmac. In theory the checkpoints are there to intercept gangsters, and with them the river of cocaine that pours continually through El Salvador. One thing the police certainly do not do is check vehicles for roadworthiness – if they did at least half the traffic would be straight off the road. Instead officers hand out spot fines for more or less imaginary infractions – for cash.

There are good things about El Salvador. It is a cheap place to live. It has a magnificent coastline, some of the Pacific Ocean's best surfing, stretches of spectacular scenery and fine Mayan ruins. Most visitors who take sensible precautions will avoid the gangs and have a good time. And the vast majority of the people are polite and friendly. They also have an engagingly dry, self-effacing sense of humour. There may even still be a few of the beautiful native red-throated hummingbirds left, along with the odd ocelot and a new generation of hippies. But the country's rainforest has shrunk to less than 2 per cent of its original size. It does still have some of the globe's most horrible insects though, including giant poisonous centipedes. I realize I am not doing the El Salvador tourist board any favours here, but these are the facts, or at least some of them.

Like its enemy, MS13 makes money from the *clicas* it controls. Many of these areas are tiny – a scattering of shacks straddling a suburban road – but they can also be city blocks and occasionally whole districts. Whatever the *clica*'s location and size, nine times out of ten the opposing gang is right across the street. Being so close to each other and general overcrowding mean that murderous gun battles break out at all times of the day and night, but especially at night. When darkness falls, rival gang members set out to hunt each other down with assault rifles, grenades, pistols, shotguns and knives.

How did these gangs come to plague El Salvador in the way they do? There are three main reasons: the first is the bloody civil war that took place between 1980 and 1992. The second is the race war waged in Los Angeles (as elsewhere in the United States) in the 1970s. That takes a little figuring out, but bear with me. The third reason is the huge gap between a small number of very wealthy haves and the extremely poor majority. These factors are closely interlinked and there are others but they will do for now.

In 1979 José Napoleon Duarte of the right-wing Christian Democratic Party led a revolutionary junta which overthrew the democratically elected President Romero. Matters rapidly deteriorated into a vicious twelve-year civil war between left and right. The terrified population suffered a wave of massacres and atrocities carried out by death squads organized and financed by both sides, but especially by El Salvador's conservative landowning right. Some 75,000 citizens died in one of the worst civil wars in human history. At one point Ronald Reagan's government was sending El Salvador's government and military $1 million a day. Cuba, Russia and Guatemala, meanwhile, supported the opposition FMLN guerrilla forces.

What has any of this got to do with the gangs? Everything. With the economy a basket case and death squads roaming the country torturing and killing at will, thousands of Salvadoreans fled to the United States. Many of them settled in south Los Angeles, but for many of these refugees it was out of the frying pan and into the fire. The LA Salvadoreans, like the Mexicans before them, found themselves caught in the interracial warfare then raging across the United States. Their response to violence at the hands of race-based gangs was to organize their own and fight back. The black LA gangs like the Bloods and the Crips might think they were tough, but their brand of thuggery mainly came down to plain old-fashioned shooting.

To get chapter and verse on this I went to meet a

couple of high-ranking MS13 gang members named Eric and Duke. We met in the shack they used as a headquarters in their home *clica*. Eric did most of the talking:

At that time, in the late seventies, early eighties, there was a race war in Los Angeles. Blacks didn't like whites, whites didn't like blacks – this shit was happening. All of a sudden we had to start defending ourselves. We were only a few of us, but we'd seen so much shit down here. When I was seven years old I used to go buy bread early in the morning and I used to find a lot of suckers decapitated by La Guardia [the police] and *los escuadrones de la muerte* – the death squads. They used to do all the dirty jobs. So we saw and we learned. Even though we didn't want to do violence, we started having to defend ourselves. We started being proud. We saw whites being proud of being white. We saw blacks being proud of being black. Why wouldn't *we* be proud of being Salvadorean?

'How did you come to be the hardest boys there?' I asked.

'Well, the thing is, gangs at that time, they used to play being a gang member. The most we can get from our rivals at those times was being stabbed or shot. That was the worst that was happening.' He shook his head.

But we didn't come from a country where we were watching somebody get stabbed. We came from a country where we were watching somebody get twenty bullets in his chest. Then his head cut off. Or his arms cut off while he was still alive. They had reached their highest violence point. And we said, 'Man, fuck this shit.' They never seen shit. Let's show them what *violence* is.

So they did. They formed MS13 and went to war. And they are still way out in front.

As a result, Mara Salvatrucha 13 and 18 Street quickly came to figure among America's – and the world's – most violent gangs, a dubious distinction they still hold today. Rapidly establishing control over their local LA turf, MS13 and 18 Street began spreading their vicious brand of gangsterism elsewhere in the United States. In no time at all they were running extortion rackets and the drugs trade with such ruthlessness that today the FBI classifies MS13 and 18 Street as 'internal terrorists'. When they catch them, the US authorities don't just prosecute the Salvadorean hoods and send them to jail, in many cases they also export them back to El Salvador. This happens in spite of the fact that by now almost all the MS13 gangsters picked up in LA and elsewhere in the United States were born there and have never set foot in El Salvador. No matter; you're in an El Salvadorean ethnic street gang, here's the special prison plane, Con Air for real. Get on it and get out.

With the United States still El Salvador's main aid donor and most important political partner – the country's official currency is the US dollar – deporting MS13 gangsters back to their 'ethnic homeland' is no problem. Every week a fresh planeload of hoods convicted in US cities on 'third strike and you're out' lands back in San Salvador to discharge its resentful cargo. Sometimes members of the two deadly rival gangs arrive on the same flight. And so a constant stream of hardened urban gangsters flows into a country already beset with one of the world's worst gang infestations.

Born and brought up in LA, bewildered gangsters suddenly find themselves deposited in a foreign country. Worried about their tattoos, some of these big hard Los Angeles gangsters are too scared to go out at night. Still, most fit right in with the rest of the gang and carry on with business as usual. Every time the streets of Los Angeles grow that little bit safer, the streets of San Salvador grow that extra bit more dangerous.

To get some idea of how *mano dura* is working – apart from its effect on the tattoo trade and clothing styles – we took a trip across country to Ciudad Barrios, one of El Salvador's maximum security prisons. When I say across country, what that actually meant was a murderous, spine-cracking, leg-numbing, deep-vein-thrombosis-inducing five-hour slog across increasingly mad, bad and dangerous roads into the heart of El Salvador's dwindling rainforest. I remember it because I drove it. When we got there, we decided that the high walls around the prison were probably not necessary: if any of the inmates did get out, it's unlikely they would get far before the fer-de-lance snakes, vipers, tarantulas or scorpions got them.

Cramped, thirsty and hungry, we stopped at the last gas station before the prison to fill up with petrol and take on supplies. Most countries do not have guards armed with shotguns at their petrol stations but in El Salvador every gas station I saw had at least one, and this one was no exception. The mosquitoes hanging around the trash cans on the forecourt were the biggest and ugliest I have ever seen, including the bee-sized variety that left my head looking like a golf ball in Alaska. Bearing in mind they carry malaria, what El Salvador's mosquitoes most make you want to do is jump straight back into your air-conditioned four-by-four and never come back out again. Except that I had already caught the disease in Africa.

And if you think the mosquitoes are big, then you should see El Salvador's flies. OK, the flies are bad in Africa. They can be terrible in parts of Australia. But as with just about everything else in this benighted country, El Salvador's flies are somehow that extra bit nastier – uglier, more persistent and capable of transmitting the kind of diseases strong men only whisper of in darkened bars. Like dengue fever, Chagas', and so on. When one of them hits you at high speed – and for some reason they all seem to be half blind – it's like being hit by a ball bearing.

I became convinced the flies were in fact part of a Mara Salvatrucha 13 outreach programme.

As I was eyeing these flying nightmares, the very worst thing that could happen to me did – I was seized by a sudden and overwhelming call of nature, the kind that frequently afflicts my sensitive English bowels in hot countries. As I stepped into what passed for the gas station's toilet, a scene straight from a horror movie met my eyes, a scene so bad I forgot to notice the terrible smell. The seat I needed so badly to use was a moving layer of blue-black flies. They swarmed over the plastic and down both sides of the pan, in what at first sight looked to be a solid mass. With dozens more of their mates on combat air patrol, there were so many flies in there the buzzing sounded like some demented orchestra tuning up for a concert. Swatting my way through the airborne sentries, I gave the toilet seat a tentative kick. Most flies in most parts of the world would take this as a hint and realize it was time to buzz off. Not this lot. Sticking fast to the seat where they lived, they just got angrier and buzzed more loudly.

Rushing outside again, I spotted an oily rag lying on the ground. Grabbing it, I charged back inside, thrashed at the seat until the bluebottles had cleared something resembling a space and plonked my butt down before the enemy could regroup. Eyes focused on some distant imaginary spot and pretending this really wasn't happening to me, I performed one of the fastest evacuations in human history. Waving goodbye with the oily rag I'd used in the absence of paper and throwing it at the enemy, I legged it out of there as fast as I could. Behind me, the massed ranks closed up and dived.

After dodging the flies and mosquitoes, it was time to go and visit some of El Salvador's human pests. Ciudad Barrios jail reared up out of the jungle before us in all its white-painted peeling ugliness. Stuck high in the middle of the rainforest, the prison was a big rectangular compound with watchtowers set at intervals along its twenty-foot-high walls. Although we were now at an elevation of some 2,000 metres and there was the usual thick blanket of cloud, the air temperature was still in the mid-thirties Celsius. Some countries force-mix rival gangsters in the belief this will somehow make them learn to love one another. If you did that in El Salvador, you would be down to single figures in a couple of months. Entrance to Ciudad Barrios is by MS13 gang membership only: it's an exclusive club. Seeing this creeper-laden *Raiders of the Lost Ark*-style scene that now opened up in front of us, Andy Thomson, our cameraman, got out and started shooting.

The guards, in black US special forces-style combats with black boots and sinister, Nazi-style shiny black gaiters, were leading examples of contemporary fascist fashion. All their weaponry was American, and they had so much of it strapped around them that to a man they walked the gorilla walk, arms akimbo and legs to match. Staring and fingering their triggers, the guards made it obvious what they were thinking: Unless you stop filming us right now, gringos, we will shoot you.

Although we had permission to enter the prison and film from the ministry of the interior, the authorities would not allow us in. At first they refused to give us a reason but after a little probing they said they were worried about the date. It was the sixth day of the sixth month of the sixth year: 666, the number of the Devil, the mark of the beast and all that. Worried that MS13 prisoners, who like to pose as satanists, might have something special prepared for us on this especially unholy day – like a big gringo barbecue – the guards rebuffed all our attempts to get in.

With nowhere else to stay, we had to turn round and head back to the capital, another five hours away over the be-nice-if-they-were-finished roads. By now it was growing dark. Just to make the day perfect, the next thing we discovered was that our driver, José, who now took the wheel, had a genuine problem seeing in the dark. We already knew he had trouble seeing in the light. And so began one of the most hair-raising journeys I have ever made, over narrow, twisting, potholed roads through the mountains with José braking too late for obstacles he had failed to spot in time. I spent most of the journey stuck to the windscreen.

We returned to Ciudad Barrios a couple of days later. This time they did let us in, but only on the strict understanding that once inside the main compound we were on our own, at our own risk and with no guarantee of help. The prison authorities could not have ensured our safety even if they'd wanted to: the guards stay outside. The prisoners manage themselves.

One thing we had failed to realize fully until now was that in El Salvador everything works on the bung. If you want something, almost anything, money has to change hands. Our failure to offer a bribe on '666 day' may have been the real reason we hadn't made it through the main gate. Now, even though we were in the administrative section of the jail and money *had* changed hands, we still had to negotiate access to the prisoners. They, and not the guards, decided who came into their domain. They also decided who came back out again.

On the way in a prison officer reminded us that if this lot were mixed in with their 18 Street rivals, the prisoners would kill each other down to the last man. About a month before we arrived, he told us, he and a couple of the other guards had noticed some of the prisoners playing football with an object that didn't look quite FIFA regulation shape and size, or bounce in the approved fashion. On taking a closer look, they found out why: it wasn't a football. Hacked from the shoulders of a suspected informer, it was a human head. About to visit hundreds of these maniacs un-guarded, this story cheered us all up no end.

There was a queue of women waiting to get into the compound with us, most of them in sexy clothes. Wives, girlfriends and prostitutes, they were waiting for a conjugal visit. These are rare and in the gift of the prison governor, but they are also a smart move: they give the men something to look forward to and help keep them in order.

I walked through the heavily barred entrance gate into the big open space I could see on the other side. There was a very competitive game of football going on. They were using a real ball. Other groups of MS13 gangsters were hanging about in what little shade they could find under the high walls, watching or talking in groups in the dusty yard. Every single one of them was facially tattooed. Most had a Devil mask.

The prison was a shit hole. The toilets, if you could call them that, were in a row to my immediate right and standing open to general view. They leaked. They were mostly blocked. They stank. And if I'd thought the flies on the outside were big, the ones in here would have been at home on the flight deck of an aircraft carrier. Going down a low wooden step to make sure the facilities were as bad as they looked, I immediately sank up to my ankles in shitty water.

The big surprise was the artwork on the compound walls. Everywhere you looked they were covered in colourful graphic graffiti of a very high standard: big, in-your-face murals in nearly every case depicting writhing, demonic women endowed with improbably pneumatic bodies, but amazingly well drawn. The other graffiti chart topper was the MS13 gang sign: the Devil's horns in the shape of the letter M.

The man who had agreed to show me round was a senior MS13 gangster named Hugo. Aged about thirty but looking much older, Hugo was a veteran who had risen to the status of *consejero*, or adviser. He was also a convicted murderer. The fact he had survived to such a ripe old age meant that in gang terms he was by definition a wise man. Patient and polite, he was the opposite of his personal bodyguard, a hulking, brute-faced mule of a man, who swaggered up, fixed me with a look that said, 'I own you, white boy, say your prayers,' and hovered at my elbow itching to do me some serious harm. Watching his fingers curl repeatedly into fists did nothing to calm my nerves. Between the brains and the brawn, I preferred the brains. Part of the US export drive, both men had been arrested on the streets of LA, flown to El Salvador, rearrested by the San Salvador police and plonked down in this filthy stinking jungle prison in the middle of nowhere, possibly for the rest of their natural lives. Imagine how happy that made them.

Everyone in the place looked tough, but Hugo's enforcer was in a league of his own. He was the type who can keep up the kind of silence that really hurts. His face and upper body were a mass of MS13 tattoos, and just in case you didn't get the message he had Devil's horns tattooed on his head. He had decided from the off that he did not like me, did not want me there and was about two heartbeats away from killing me. There is only one way of dealing with this kind of problem. Turning to him and meeting his gaze I asked, 'Have I upset you?'

The key thing, as always, is to relax the shoulders, soften the face and show no fear. Once they see or smell fear on you, then you might as well forget it. It would have caused them problems to harm us, and these prisoners already had more than enough problems to be going on with, but in a prison like Ciudad Barrios when you are doing 400 years what have you got to lose?

The enforcer finally opened his mouth. 'You remind me of a policeman who used to beat me up when I was a kid in south LA.' Just my luck.

Now that we had broken the ice, I took a moment to check out my admirer's body art. It was women, women and more women, naked or half-naked beauties who looked as if they had been inflated with a bicycle pump. The tattoos, which I suddenly realized represented the enforcer's real girlfriends, showed them in sexually suggestive poses with their names next to them. Except for the last one on this fleshy roll of honour, all the names had been crossed out with a thick black line and BITCH tattooed alongside in capital letters. That's the thing about love: with the best will in the world, some relationships just don't work out.

I noticed straight away that the American MS13 gangsters like these two showing me round the prison took precedence over the local boys. Just as they ran much of the gang's business, the deportees looked like they ran Ciudad Barrios penitentiary. The local hoods did as they were told, sticking to a strict and scarily well-organized hierarchy. The MS13 command and control structure seemed far better than that of the local police.

Hugo and the Hulk took me to a corner of the yard where there was a tap and turned it on. The water was filthy – a luminous green trickle that looked as if it harboured every serious disease on the face of the earth, from cholera to dysentery and plenty in between. And in fact, Hugo told me, the prisoners were often ill, mostly with bad stomach upsets. The water, Hugo hinted, was the only reason the gang had let me and the crew film them. By using my influence as a well-known gringo (I don't know why they thought I had any), MS13 hoped I could somehow convince the prison authorities to pipe in the cool, clean water they dreamed about.

With the enforcer sticking to me like an ugly shadow, Hugo and I met more of the inmates. As we talked I realized something else. Here, in this pit, the gangsters were fashion conscious. There was a look. Almost all of them were wearing knee-length surfer-style shorts, smart trainers and snazzy-coloured T-shirts. But the most amazing thing was their socks, which were blazing white, like adverts for soap powder. And now that I was beginning to relax and take in the scenery a bit more, I saw there was washing hanging everywhere. Despite the mud, the dust, the excrement and the disgusting water, even here in this desperate dump these men were doing their best to keep up standards. I suppose it helped them get through the day. The basic food they eat is eggs, tomatoes, cheese and beans, spiced up with chilli and anything else they can get. And more eggs, tomatoes, cheese and beans ... The men cooked for themselves in small groups on ancient stoves powered by liquid gas, and had to buy their food either out of their own pockets or with shared MS13 gang funds. They slept in long, narrow and extremely cramped dormitories.

It wasn't just MS13's tight organization that impressed me; the other striking thing was the way these guys gave each other support, loyalty and protection. It was a cooperative community. They didn't just pool their money for food and take turns with the cooking and chores; Hugo said they took care of one another when they were ill. There was little or no official medical care. They were as tight-knit as a close family, in some ways even tighter. They had to be, to survive in there. There was no evidence of the systematic violence and bullying that I'd come across in other prisons I had visited in the course of the series.

As we went a little further and the full horror of Ciudad Barrios sank ever deeper into my brain, I could feel myself ageing physically. There was something so crushing about the place that beat me down and kept on beating. The dirt and disease, the smell, the alternating dust and mud, the flies, the water, the heat and humidity, the total lack of privacy, the tattoos everywhere reminding you of where you were, why you were in there, the loved one back in Los Angeles you would never see again. I don't know how the prisoners could stand being in there for a single day, and I'm not at all certain I could last any time before wanting to do something drastic like find a length of rope and a beam to go with it. To take my mind off the grimness I asked Hugo, 'Do you have any family on the outside?'

'Sure,' he said. 'I got my son in Los Angeles – he's fourteen.'

I took a bit of a chance with the next question. 'Will he become a member of MS13?'

To my surprise, Hugo was not fazed. 'No. I tell him not to hang around with gangsters. I tell him do his school work and grow up good.' He knew and I knew Hugo was never going to see his son again. Abruptly changing the subject, he told me how an American news journalist who had made a programme about Ciudad Barrios had claimed MS13 threatened to kidnap her. Back in the US, this had made a big splash. Now Hugo had the media to himself, in the shape of me and Andy, he wanted to seize his moment. 'If MS13 had wanted to kidnap her, we would have done it. Don't make a big deal about nearly getting kidnapped. Wait till you *get* kidnapped. If you live through it, *then* you can shout about it.'

I looked at him to see if they had anything along

these lines planned for me, but he was just making a general point.

Once they have been deported and locked up under *mano dura*, for most of these guys that's the end of the line. Some of them have 1,000-year sentences. If by some fluke they are released, most of them try to get straight back into the US, where they have homes, families and an established way of life. And pizzas and steaks and movies instead of a constant diet of cheese and beans eaten looking at twenty-foot-high Devil-graffitied walls. But having previously been deported, they are viewed by the US authorities as illegal immigrants. The chances are they'd be picked up and exiled for the second time. With all of their options closed down, what's left for these men? They have the gang; they have each other. That's all. That's why they stay so tight.

In an effort to contain the mayhem, the police carry out sporadic raids on gang houses. El Salvador police raids are not like our own, where at the worst a few dozen officers might come round your gaff with a battering ram and smash their way in. That's bad enough, but when the law comes to call in El Salvador we're talking full-scale mechanized warfare: blitzkrieg, only without the dive-bombing. To impress us with their diligence and purpose, the police invited us to join them on a night raid.

Designed to 'seal off a notorious *clica* and search

it for drugs, dealers, weapons, money and gang foot soldiers', the party I joined involved a mixed force of some 500 heavily armed SWAT police plus army infantry. It looked as if we were about to invade neighbouring Honduras, not go on a drugs bust. As we drove up to the police station I thought a coup against the government was about to go down. I sincerely hoped for the sake of my new-found gang acquaintances that the *clica* in question was not up the end of a disused railway track. Dressing for business, most of the men – and they were all men – donned masks for the usual reason. Then we waited. For hours. By this time it was late at night and it was raining – one of the worst, most torrential downpours I have ever experienced. Even the police officers, who aren't told the names of the target in advance in case they tip them off, didn't know what the hell was going on. Some were worried they might be going into their own neighbourhoods. Only a handful of senior officers knew the target until a few seconds before the 'Go' command.

We shot off at high speed, in my own case in the back of a Datsun pickup. Now that we were moving, the rain was like a hail of twenty-pence pieces – with no protective clothing and only a black T-shirt between me and it. But as we charged through the streets, slicing through the traffic in the convoy with APCs and hundreds of armed troops, their regulation black ponchos glistening in the driving rain and their rifle barrels gleaming in the city lights, it was hard not to feel a part of it. So I did. Five hundred heavily armed men and me, roaring out to take down a bunch of gangsters, is some buzz. All we needed was 'The Ride of the Valkyries' on the loudspeakers and a couple of helicopter gunships for company to get the full *Apocalypse Now* effect. So I started humming it. This started Andy off laughing.

By the time we reached our top-secret first target, a heavily fortified drugs outlet, there was a scrum of TV news teams on the spot, already up and filming. The target had unaccountably been leaked to the press – those strict 'need-to-know' security precautions must have fallen down somewhere. Quite possibly as a result of something that folded ending up in someone's back pocket. The target house was enclosed from top to bottom in an iron cage, with bars and grilles extending right up to roof level. The seedy, ramshackle building was like a classic Los Angeles crack house and then some. To gain entry, the police had to climb the front of the cage and cut through the bars on the first floor with oxyacetylene torches.

Naturally, this all took some time. Explosives would have been useful. By the time the MOE (methods of entry) specialists had got the assault elements of the task force inside, four of the six men they had hoped to arrest had already fled into the storm. Of the others, one was lying face down on the floor in the living room. His underpants were brown, he was that scared. But the gangster wasn't alone: with his eye glued to the camera, Andy stepped in a drain and sank in the sewage up to his ankles. Being a cameraman carries with it all kinds of unforeseeable risks.

The raid was an anticlimax, not to say a journalistic free-for-all. But as we walked out into the driving rain, looking forward to our comfortable hotel beds, I couldn't help asking myself what the poor sods living round here made of it all. If you saw 500 heavily armed men coming after your neighbours in the UK, you might conclude you were no longer living in a lawful or safe society. And you would be right. That's the problem with gangs: once they take hold, it is very, very difficult to root them out, no matter how hard you try.

Before we joined the raid I had been invited to meet a government official with specific responsibility for tackling drug trafficking. I didn't warm to this man, who wished to remain anonymous, and I certainly didn't trust him. He told me that the cocaine trade was controlled entirely by the *clica* gangs. As far as he was concerned, all El Salvador's problems began and ended with people like the Small Psychopaths. 'With the help of US advisers and American financial and military aid,' he said, 'the El Salvador government is doing everything in its power to end both this and the power of the gangs.' The second I met this man, it was crystal clear to me that if I asked him any challenging questions at all, then not only would we not be allowed to go on any more drugs raids, we'd be on the next flight out of the country. So I kept shtum, nodded and smiled at everything he told me and tried to look happy.

Cameras are heavy, awkward things. As we were leaving, by way of thanks for our host's cooperation, Andy accidentally swung our camera into the plate glass that formed one wall of his palatial office. There was a faint tinkling sound and a small star-shaped mark appeared in the centre of the glass. Then, as we stood watching in fascinated horror, a long, jagged split began to crawl out from the point of impact, followed by another and another, spreading as they do in a *Tom and Jerry* cartoon, until, with an almighty crash, the entire wall fell apart and smashed into shards on the tiled floor. Optimistic as ever, Andy took out some gaffer tape and offered to stick it back together. Grabbing him, we left our host standing there staring at the remains of his office.

If I'd had trouble believing everything the government official told me, my next interviewee confirmed my doubts. An ex-intelligence officer, Lionel Gomez was now an 'adviser' on El Salvador with powerful connections in and ties to the US Senate. The interview took place at his house, which was built like Fort Knox. A heavyset man in his early fifties with a broad fleshy face and small round spectacles, Gomez let me know he had at least one very attractive twenty-two-year-old Salvadorean girlfriend and possibly more. He also had an office decked with photographs of himself chewing the fat with Senator Edward Kennedy, President Gorbachev, Fidel Castro and various other global bigwigs, and a nice line in seen-it-all-before spook world-weariness. He would have been right at home in a Graham Greene novel. The white coffee mug stamped with CIA on his desk might just have been a hint about his former job. Someone's man in San Salvador, he definitely wasn't selling vacuum cleaners.

Without going as far as to say the government controlled the narcotics trade, Gomez explained that the MS13 and 18 Street gangs provided useful cover for the real masters of the cocaine trade in El Salvador: the nameless powerful figures I was never going to meet who would kill me and the entire crew if we ever did bump into them.

'Everybody will tell you the *clicas* are involved in drugs – dealing drugs, moving them. But there's a problem with that: according to the DEA 570 tonnes of pure cocaine go through El Salvador every year.'

I stopped Gomez to make sure I had heard him right. 'Five hundred and seventy tonnes?'

'Tonnes. Of cocaine. Pure cocaine. This could be worth $30,000,000,000. The *clicas* are not doing that. They wouldn't live the way they live if they were moving 570 tonnes of cocaine. In order for the big business to exist and move about in an efficient way, it is necessary to have the ambience, the society of corruption. So it's very useful to have *clicas*, because it catches the attention of the press, and it's very flamboyant because of the tattoos. But the real story is the guys who move the 570 tonnes.'

'So who are they?'

'Well,' he said in his slow Spanish-accented drawl, 'I would say some of the most powerful people in the region.'

'People in the government? Businessmen?'

Gomez nodded. 'Maybe, yes.'

'So the biggest gang in the country is the government?'

'Yes. But they don't wear tattoos. They wear Rolex watches and very expensive ties.'

'What you're saying is, it suits them to have gang warfare going on as a smokescreen and that takes everybody's eye off the fact that what they're doing is shipping all this cocaine through the country.'

Gomez just looked at me.

'But if the corruption is so obvious, why doesn't anybody do anything about it?'

He looked at me again for a second or two and then replied, 'Fear. They kill you. They can starve you to death. They can shoot you. Or you could have an "accident" done by one of the *clicas*. They can steal your wallet in the street and shoot you. This is a very casual country when it comes to violence.'

Having spent time in the *clicas* I could see the force of his argument. If Gomez is right, El Salvador is the main conduit for the supply of cocaine to the entire western United States, Canada and the Pacific. The whole raid had probably been little more than a show of strength – with the emphasis on 'show' – to convince El Salvador's television viewers, along with any powerful foreign observers who happened to be watching, that the government meant business. If there were gangsters getting arrested for drug trafficking live on the nightly TV news then, hey, the government must be doing its best. It cannot possibly be to blame for the cocaine economy.

When we got back to my hotel after the interview with Gomez I found an urgent message waiting from Chucho the Small Psychopath. He wanted help. His wife, Ingrid, was in Susaltepeque, San Salvador's MS13 female prison, originally for selling marijuana but now for her alleged role in a prison murder. As with the men, female gang members are segregated into either MS13 or 18 Street jails. Since the chances of his being arrested were extremely high if he stepped outside his home *clica*, Chucho asked if I would help him get in to see both Ingrid and his little daughter. The toddler had been born in prison and was locked up with Ingrid. In El Salvador imprisoning small children with their mothers is seen as more humane than the system in the UK, under which mother and child are separated and the children often put into care.

We stuck Chucho in the back of our hired MPV, told him to keep his head down and picked up his sister Maria and his mother on the way. Maria, a short buxom teenager with big hair and a smile to go with it, immediately took a shine to me. Gringos are targeted by local women desperate to get out of the country and live somewhere with fewer gangsters. This may have had more to do with it than my personal charms, but I wouldn't want to sound too cynical. At any rate, as soon as the opportunity arose Maria bought me a big stuffed toy bear. It was the kind you win at fairgrounds, except that she had drowned this particular animal in perfume. Racked with violence, in El Salvador stuffed animals are something of a national passion, especially with the women, who seem to use them as a kind of comfort blanket. God knows, they need one. Not quite sure what to do or say, I later gave Maria a big stuffed toy in return. This was the worst thing I could have done, as it signalled undying love between the two of us. Luckily I had the foresight to give her my present as we were leaving for the airport.

We reached Susaltepeque. Our researcher, Marta Shaw, had gone in to set the prison visit up. She had been cavity-searched. The guards who had searched her were female, but they didn't wear sterile surgical gloves as they do in the UK. They used plastic shopping bags from the local supermarket, and they used them regardless of whether they had already been employed for shopping. And they recycled them. This isn't very hygienic. Or very comfortable, from Marta's account.

Now we were there, it was our turn. En route across town, the main topic of conversation in the MPV was the inevitable 'Who's going to get cavity-searched first?' Since the whole *Gangs* series was my idea in the first place, it seemed churlish not to volunteer. A guard showed me into a bare, strip-lit room furnished with a table, a chair and a second guard in the corner armed with an automatic rifle whose expression was the most wooden thing in the room. The first guard, I assumed, was the person who was going to delve into my bits.

Keen to get the ordeal over and done with, I undid my belt, dropped my trousers and underpants and stood there waiting for him to get on with it. The guard's eyes bulged from his head, and then a furious frown replaced his astonished expression. In a mixture of Spanish and English he demanded, 'What is the matter with you? Are you mad or *loco*?'

Bewildered to say the least, I stared back at him. Then it dawned on me: there wasn't going to be any cavity search. By some amazing stroke of luck we had been excused shopping bags. But there I was standing with my trousers and pants round my ankles, ready for action. As I hurriedly pulled up my trousers, he thrust a round wooden disc with a number painted on it into my hand. 'This is your ID number for when you are in prison,' he said hoarsely. 'Keep it with you at all times.' Tapping his temple with a forefinger, he motioned for me to leave. As I went, he spluttered, 'You loco, gringo. Loco.' Looking back, I'm inclined to agree with him. The moral of the story is, never drop your pants before you are asked – especially in a prison.

Generously deciding to share some of my deep humiliation with the team, I put on the kind of bent-legged, limping walk you might adopt when you really have had a plastic bag shoved up you, and assumed an agonized expression to go with it. Andy and Antony were waiting anxiously outside.

'How was it?' Antony asked.

Staggering up and leaning on him as if for support, I croaked, 'It's OK, really – it's just that my throat's a bit tight.'

Antony stared at me in undisguised horror. My throat? Had they really shoved the bag up that far? 'Right,' he said. 'That's it. I'm not going in. You'll have to do this one on your own.'

Cracking a smile, I told him the happy truth: we were cool.

We knew in advance that this was an all-female prison, but it was still really bizarre to see upwards of 400 captive women in this big, mould-streaked, high-ceilinged Dickensian dive – and, as a male, to walk around in there freely. The surreal nature of the experience was heightened by the fact that in the background we could hear Queen's 'Bohemian Rhapsody' playing over the internal tannoy system. Chucho – who was touchingly dressed up in his Sunday best – fell on his wife's neck, then took his little girl on his knee and gave her a big hug and a kiss. It was the first time he had ever seen her, and while his daughter just cried Chucho cried tears of joy.

When the song's guitar solo came round, Antony and I launched into a rather bad impression of Brian May, giving our air guitar solo. When the track ended, hordes of women crowded round us, cheering and clapping and demanding an encore. The local male visitors did not share their wives' and girlfriends' enthusiasm. In fact, they were mightily pissed off: they had bribed, pleaded and made all that effort to get in there, only to find their women more interested in two loco gringos.

Chucho's mother now launched into a solo of her own, a long litany of family woe. Unsure whether to laugh or cry at seeing her little granddaughter for the first time, she reminded no one in particular that she had already lost a son, a husband, a brother, a cousin and a daughter-in-law in the gangs. The way things were headed, she was likely to lose her other son. To cheer her up, Chucho told his mum all the right things: how he'd get out of the gang and go straight, how Ingrid and the kid would get out of prison and everything would be all right. None of us believed a blind word of this, least of all Chucho's mother, but it helped make things better for the time being. It was like putting a Band-Aid on a broken arm.

The bad news for Chucho's wife was that she was being held indefinitely on suspicion of conspiracy to murder. Which meant that she and the little girl might be in there for a very long time. Just as Ingrid was completing her sentence for possession of marijuana a new MS13 prisoner had been brought in to Susaltepeque. There are cells for inmates, but most of the women find a bed space wherever they can in the large communal dormitories. In other words, there is no place to hide. The new girl was suspected of informing on fellow MS13 gang members to the police so a group of women – allegedly including Ingrid – stabbed her to death.

As time went on I began to see that in El Salvador the middle class is still a work in progress. It is mainly the haves against the have-nots, except that there a lot of the have-nots not only have guns, they are only too ready and willing to use them. You hear people complaining about the British class system and recently social mobility seems to have gone into reverse, but given a choice between life in the UK and life in El Salvador, I'm for the pushy, competitive but law-abiding British middle classes every time.

Anxious to find something positive to say about El Salvador, my next stop was Granja Escuela, an up-country rehabilitation centre for female gang members. A former government research centre that had fallen on hard times, this was a low-rise, rambling series of buildings stuck out in the middle of the bush about two hours' drive from the capital. A counterpart to *mano dura, mano amiga* (helping hand) is a ramshackle and ill-administered government scheme that aims to give fourteen women at a time the chance to quit the gangs and get back into mainstream society. The only place in El Salvador where 18 Street and MS13 gangsters mingle in the same place, Granja Escuela offers a six-part course that includes basic education, manual skills, spiritual counselling, family support, a bit of a brush with the arts and some sport. It also offers a temporary refuge from the gangs. Rapidly sinking back into the rainforest from which it had risen, the place resounded to the calls of forest birds. Dozens of chickens scratched around and clucked in the lush green vegetation, there to provide the eggs that seemed to form the staple of most Salvadorean dishes.

When we showed up, the latest Granja Escuela intake were busy baking beautiful little biscuits and cakes for the bakery business they wanted to set up. But what had really pulled them into this place, I now learned, was the laser tattoo removal machine on the premises. It had been supplied by the US Agency for International Development (USAID), which describes itself as 'an independent agency that provides economic, development and humanitarian assistance around the world in support of the foreign policy goals of the United States'. The chance to get rid of their tattoos was the main reason the women were there.

All in their teens or early twenties, they seemed like bright, friendly, lively people, the kind you might hope to meet anywhere. Except, that is, for their eyes, which in every case held the same cold flat knowledge of killing and death as their male counterparts. In return for letting us film them, they'd told Marta Shaw they wanted only one thing – make-up. But it couldn't be any old make-up; it had to be pancake theatrical-strength foundation that would cover just about anything. This was hard to come by in El Salvador, and at twenty dollars a pot not affordable. They also wanted make-up remover. Without really wondering why they might need all this stuff we agreed to the deal.

Seated around one of the long tables, we got chatting in the big, friendly kitchen where they baked their cakes and biscuits. When I was a kid, my mum ran a small hairdressing salon, so I grew up liking the company of women. One after another, while mosquitoes the size of small birds buzzed around us looking for an opportunity to suck our blood, the gang women told me their stories. Of the thirteen girls who had started this particular course six weeks previously, only eleven were still alive. One had accidentally electrocuted herself – she'd touched a power cable with a metal pole, trying to knock down some mangoes in the grounds. The other had been shot dead by a rival gang when she went back home to see her family for the weekend.

It turned out that Granja Escuela only offers refuge during the week – come Friday the women have to go back to the *clicas*. Of the eleven, two had been deported from Los Angeles while the rest had grown up in San Salvador. Most of them had babies and young children in tow. As long as they were up here in the jungle they were relatively safe. The minute they set foot back in the *clicas* they risked death and retribution from their respective gangs – not least for cooperating with the hated government.

The first woman I spoke to, 'Angela', told me how as a girl of fifteen she'd been cornered one morning and told she had to join the gang. She refused. Eighteen women set about her, slapping, punching and kicking her to the ground. After this *castigo*, or punishment, the men arrived. They held Angela down and took turns raping her. When the men had finished, the women forcibly tattooed Angela, covering the skin of her forehead and cheeks with big crudely drawn versions of the 18 Street logo. Since then Angela had been held as the gang's common property, subject to any kind of abuse by any 18 Street gang member at any time. Looking into her eyes as we talked, I could see the depth and strength of the misery and utter devastation this had caused this young woman. Without warning Angela began to cry, in silence and without changing her expression. Inside, where it counted, Angela was broken.

One woman showed me her disfigured arm – she had tried to remove her gang tattoo with a piece of molten plastic and a knife. Even if girls did agree to join the gang, she said, and chose a beating instead of the train at initiation, the men would still rape them. With the police only entering the *clicas* in overpowering force and at widely spaced intervals, the only law was the law of the jungle.

Once in the gang, these women had to do the same

jobs as the men, including armed robbery, extortion and assassination. How did she feel about committing murder? The woman shrugged. 'A mission is a mission. It has to be done. If you don't do the mission, they shoot you.'

'Have you killed anyone?'

She giggled. 'Yes. Perhaps many times.'

This invited the question, so I asked it: Who had killed someone? 'Can you put your hands up?'

One by one, they raised their hands. I was in a room full of murderers. Again. For me this was the defining moment of my time in El Salvador. The way this twenty-four-year-old woman admitted to murder was so matter of fact, and so chilling.

Many bizarre things happened while we were in this strange place. The women didn't just tell tales of horror from the *clicas*; they joked, they messed about. Stuck out here in the wilds, having visitors, especially new male visitors, was a bit of a treat for them. But what impressed me most about these women was that they were so honest, so frank and so direct. They told the truth.

Even with all that I had learned, I was totally unprepared for what happened next. As if at an unspoken signal, each of the women in the room reached for the make-up remover we had bought for them. The first took a small ball of cotton wool. Slowly she began swabbing her face. Underneath the thick make-up they had applied before we showed up, their faces were a mass of black glaring tattoos. Surely no laser machine in the world had a chance in hell of removing them. In a moment these funny and charming women had become different people: the bad people you fear on sight, criminals you would go a long way to avoid. In the warmth of our conversation I had forgotten where these women came from and why they were there.

Though I tried, it was impossible to hide the way I felt. And as they watched my own expression change, their faces fell too. All the fun and life that had been in them just a moment before bled away. As I was getting ready to leave, a woman who had been forced to join 18 Street came up to me. Putting a finger to the skin of her cheeks, she said, 'They put a gun in my mouth while they did this.'

There were two other sad things about the Granja Escuela project. The first was that the tattoo removal machine was broken and no one knew how to fix it. The second that if the El Salvador government – or for that matter USAID – set up a series of similar full-time residential programmes with removal machines that actually worked, they could probably reduce gang numbers significantly. A lot of people, not just the women, want to get out. The facial tattoos mean they never can.

As a way of saying thank you, I left money for enough make-up to last them six months. It seemed like the least I could do. In El Salvador an eighteen-dollar bottle of make-up can save your life. As we made our way back towards the car park, Angela stopped me with a tug on the sleeve. 'Sir,' she said in Spanish, 'I want to speak to you.' Calling for Marta to translate, I waited. Very simply, Angela said, 'Thank you for treating us like women.' I turned and walked along the path to our vehicle. El Salvador is a country that continually tugs at your heart strings.

As we had learned on our first day in the country, you don't have to go very far in El Salvador to come across a dead body. On the way back to town we spotted more police activity by the roadside and again stopped. Making our way up a dirt track, we came across a cordoned-off crime scene. Officers were photographing two bodies. The men's shoes had been taken off, but they still had their socks on. The investigating coroner had just arrived.

There were signs of torture on the half-naked bodies, particularly the small grey-black marks of cigarette burns. Shot through the forehead, a bullet had blown off the back of the first man's skull. Black flies were busy in the red and grey mess. He had been twenty years old. A second corpse, his twenty-one-year-old brother, had already been bagged up and placed in the back of a flatbed truck. He too had been tortured after going missing the night before. The police told me the brothers had run a bus service for the local people, trying to make their way in life with one ancient bus that they operated on a shoestring. It had been hard for them to make money, he said, not least because they had been paying the 18 Street gang a 'toll' for using a section of road.

The evening before the killings, a group of 18 Street members had come calling to demand yet more money. The brothers had refused to pay the increased toll for the simple reason they could not afford it. That night they had been abducted, tortured and then killed. Both made to kneel, one brother had been forced to watch as the gang tortured and then shot the second, before he was tortured and shot in his turn.

The murdered men's mother was there. She was screaming. It was a high-pitched wail, the kind you only ever hear at the scene of car crashes or at funerals, like an animal losing its cubs. I felt sick. It was one of the very few times in the series I wanted the camera to stop. I asked Andy to turn it off. He quite rightly ignored me – rightly, because showing the reality of what gangs can do was what we were there for. We didn't film as much as we might have done.

The words rang in my head: 'A mission is a mission.' These two innocent, hard-working kids, cut down for the sake of a few bucks a week. A mother's life destroyed. After the bodies had been removed we walked up to where the brothers had spent their last moments on earth. The imprint of their bodies and some of the blood, brains and skull where they had died, eye to eye, were still there on the grass.

*

Just before we left for the airport, we heard that Groupie had gone into hiding. Word was he had shot dead his sister, the very sister he had lived with all his life and who had helped raise him. He thought she was going out with an 18 Street member. Groupie had gone after the 18 Street guy and mistakenly shot his sister. Now his own gang were out to kill him.

We also heard that Chucho had allegedly been involved in the group rape of a female minor.

On the road out we passed a strange sculpture. A figure symbolizing justice had been placed beside the road. Our local driver called her the 'lady with the big boobies'. She was naked and had large breasts. In one hand she held the sword of justice, in the other she was meant to have the scales. But someone probably with first-hand experience of El Salvador's judicial system had removed them. For me it just about summed up the country's sense of humour.

Chucho, Joker and Groupie are all in prison, serving long sentences.

4. St Louis

This is a sad thing to say, but if you were new to the city of St Louis and wanted to make some money, you could do a lot worse than go into the soft toy trade. Wherever I went in the poor parts of the city, I saw stuffed bears tied to street signs, lamp posts and palings. In Europe we generally say it with flowers, but here every time a young gangster dies his relatives and friends fix a fluffy toy – usually a brightly coloured bear – near the spot where he or she fell. Since gang-bangers are shot, stabbed and otherwise murdered all too often in the city of St Louis, there's a brisk market in mementos. Why fluffy toys? Because so many of those who die are still teenagers – kids snatched from their families before they have even had time to grow up. Too young to vote, too young to drink, but not too young to fall to a volley of drive-by bullets or in a gang ambush. Like so many modern totems, the lamp post tributes are sad statements of loss – the loss of a city's young men and women to gang violence.

A quick chat with the local police in the shape of Sergeant Carlos Ross, head of the St Louis police department's gang unit, made it painfully clear that beautiful, laid-back St Louis is one of the most dangerous cities in the US. The Bloods and the Crips have been at war in its northern and eastern districts for longer than twenty years; now, I learned from Sergeant Ross, both gangs are trying to expand south.

Styling itself the Gateway to the West, St Louis is a vast city that curls languidly along the west bank of the mighty Mississippi. Steaming hot in summer – when we were there – and freezing cold in winter, a better name for it these days might be Gateway to the Gangs. There have always been gangs in St Louis – Jesse James operated not too far away in Clay County, Missouri, and there were some fearsome Irish and Italian gangs bootlegging here during the Prohibition years.

But modern mobsters are much deadlier than the early models – not least because the city is awash with firearms. Assault rifles, sub-machine guns, shotguns and automatic pistols are two a penny, and they are all far more accurate – and much more reliable – than weapons were in the days of the Wild West. They also have a much higher rate of fire and even the ammo's better. The St Louis authorities estimate that some 8,000 gangsters are currently at large in the greater metropolitan area, which means the gangs are much bigger and more widespread than they used to be.

This isn't going to win me many Missourian friends, but in St Louis, despite the fact that black–white relations generally in the US are way better than they were, the sense of racial division struck me hard. The more affluent, mainly white suburbs are in the south;

the poorer, and this means the mainly black areas, are to the north and east. When I asked them about this, most locals looked at their shoes for a couple of seconds and then admitted it was true. The unofficial dividing line is the lively Delmar Boulevard, with its trendy shops and top restaurants and clubs. It slices through the city from east to west, marking a kind of demilitarized zone between rich and poor.

The downtown area is a nice confection of eighteenth-century French and nineteenth-century Victorian architecture, some of it restored, some 're-created'. Hardly anybody in the city speaks French any more, but for sentimental and touristic reasons the people cling to the city's heritage as a French colonial trading centre. What they don't cling to and would like to forget is the disaster that hit the US motor manufacturing trade towards the end of the last millennium. The city's manufacturing industry collapsed. Employing thousands of mainly blue-collar workers, the engineering plants that built the machines that kept the vehicles rolling off the production lines in Detroit all closed down in the space of a few years. Better-built, more fuel-efficient foreign cars were grabbing the market from American gas-guzzler cars and trucks. As the plants closed, the jobs and the people went with them: thousands moved out to seek work elsewhere, triggering a 40 per cent fall in the city's population between 1960 and 2000. The flight gave rise to jobless urban blight, with empty homes rotting where they stood.

But St Louis is fighting back. Where there are large empty homes for sale at knock-down prices, there will be people anxious to buy them. And not everyone is inclined to join a gang. Over the past decade or so a whole new wave of immigrants has started to repopulate some of the run-down districts that have fuelled gang culture. Including hundreds of Bosnian and Serb refugees from the civil war in former Yugoslavia, the vast majority are hard-working entrepreneurs. There are signs the incomers are starting to turn things around – opening shops and small businesses, populating the schools with new blood, paying their taxes and obeying the law. New corporations are arriving to replace the old, especially in the health and pharmaceutical sectors. Is it time to get out the bunting and celebrate? Not going by the most recent levels of recorded crime. But there is hope that some real change for the better is taking root.

Driving around the worst of the city's districts, at first glance you think the big, imposing red-brick Addams Family-style houses with their turrets, finials and generous back gardens still play home to 1950s happy families, where Dad goes off to work, Mom does the home baking and the kids do their homework. But get up close and you see that ceilings have fallen in, windows are broken and gardens are a mass of waist-high weeds. Quite often, large trees are growing up through the roofs. They look as if they have been hit by one of the JDAM bombs Boeing manufactures in the city. The crumbling brick shells make it feel as if whole swathes of the city are dying. They are, and the young gang members who haunt them and use them to hide guns and drugs in are dying too.

The particular death we focused on for the programme was the murder of Robert Lee Walker. A good-looking, easy-going seventeen-year-old with striking eyes and a three-month-old son named Elijah by his girlfriend Courtney, Walker was close to graduating from St Louis Learning Center South High School. He wanted to be an architect. On his way home on the bus from school on the afternoon of Friday 5 May 2006 Walker signalled the driver to stop at the corner of Lillian and Emerson, near his home in Walnut Park in the extreme north-west of the city. A friend and his cousin got off the bus with him.

A gang of armed teenagers waited in ambush. Guns blazing, they rushed Walker and his two friends. Trapped against the side of the bus, Walker went down in a hail of bullets. Shot through the body, shoulders and arms, he was probably bleeding to death when a bullet went in through the back of his head and exited between his eyes. Whether or not it was a deliberate execution shot, it guaranteed his death. Walker's friend and his cousin survived with minor injuries. The driver, who had superficial lacerations from flying glass, raced his bullet-ridden bus to the nearest police station. The boy charged with the murder is just fifteen years old.

Killings like this don't just end a single life; they

shatter whole families, undermine communities and drag all of us back down the ladder a step. When we went to visit Robert Walker's mother, Arthella Spence, who lived in a run-down, timber-framed house close to where the killing took place, she insisted that her son was not and never had been a gang member. But Sergeant Ross of the gang unit told me he suspects there may have been some involvement. Union Boulevard, two blocks west of the bus stop where Walker was murdered, marks the front line between two warring gangs. The 49 Bad Bloods lay claim to the 4,900 city blocks of Beacon, Alcott and Davison Avenues. The Geraldine Street Crips haunt a typically dilapidated neighbourhood on the other side of the Mark Twain Expressway.

Nobody except the gangs themselves understands exactly what they are fighting about from day to day, but feuds are usually over control of the drugs trade. Whatever the reason, the day before Walker's murder the escalating violence boiled over when a group of 49 Bad Bloods allegedly shot dead a Geraldine Street Crip nicknamed Four-Foot. Whether the Bloods really did kill Four-Foot is irrelevant to Walker's fate. The Crips believed the 49 Bads had done it, and macho gang pride – known around here by one of the deadliest words in the English language, respect – dictated that a Blood had to pay in the same coin. When the Crips came looking for payback it seems they found Robert Lee Walker. What's really hard for an outsider like me to understand is that Walker may well have been killed simply for being in the wrong place at the wrong time.

Was Robert Walker a Bloods foot soldier, a fighting member who went out armed and took on Crips like Four-Foot? It doesn't look like it. The day before his murder Robert had mowed the lawns of the Walnut Park Bible Church he attended every Sunday morning with his mother. He also sang in the church choir. But as far as Sergeant Ross is concerned, none of that cuts much ice: Ross says Walker was known to his gang unit as a 49 Bad fellow-traveller. He may not have pulled any triggers and he may have gone to church with his mom, but he probably hung around the 'hood with the wrong sort of brethren, the sort who dress in red, the universal Bloods gang colour.

Sure enough, at Walker's funeral a few days later many of the more than 300 mourners turned up wearing red. Mostly teenagers, lots of them left Robert farewell notes like '4 Eva Missed'. Friends also tied red teddy bears and red balloons to lamp posts, fences and trees, left Walker, or Li'l Robert as they called him, messages inked on red bandannas and spray-painted red graffiti on neighbouring walls. Some of the graffiti promised bloody revenge on the Crips. Messages like 'Life Blood Gang' and 'R.I.P. Homeboy' suggest that Walker may have been slightly more than a choirboy; 'homeboy' is one of the many slang terms for a gangster.

Whatever the truth, a young boy has been brutally murdered and his family left grieving. The family's only breadwinner, Arthella Spence works in a St Louis retirement home as a care assistant. When I spoke to her there were no men around – Robert had been the only male, and now even he was gone. Devastated by her son's death, Spence no longer cooks for her remaining family. With tears streaming down her face, tears that moved me almost as much as they did her family, she said, 'Robert always loved what I cooked for him, always ate all of it down to the last crumb. Now he's gone, I don't got the heart to make no more food.' She told me how she had written a poem about the murder and sent it to a Web-based company purporting to run a poetry competition. The company emailed her back to say that her poem had won a prize, and in return for the sum of twenty dollars they would send her a certificate to prove it. The certificate hung in pride of place on the living-room wall. 'You see,' Spence said proudly, 'I'm a poet.'

Every day, unable to go near the spot where her son was murdered, she makes a long detour that puts two extra miles on her walk to work. Afraid the same fate might befall her remaining children, Arthella has decided to move away from Walnut Park to a house in a less gang-infested district of St Louis owned by her brother. The memories are too bad to live with – but her flight means another empty house will join the rest that are crumbling away. Courtney, Robert's sixteen-year-old girlfriend, is also quitting the district, determined to make a better, safer life.

Listening to Spence's story I realized that it is almost impossible for kids like Robert to escape the gangs. Gang culture is like an invisible fog that gets everywhere and affects everything, even down to what you can and can't wear. It's like living under an evil spell. Where I grew up, most people supported West Ham. If you happened to support another football team, you didn't wear its colours except on match day – it just wasn't worth the aggravation. Common sense, you might say, but even these days on Britain's streets it's hard to imagine someone getting shot – murdered – by a Chelsea fan for wearing the Arsenal strip in public. In St Louis, as in south LA, the colour on your back can be a matter of life or death. Most people wear the neighbourhood gang colour just to be on the safe side. The irony is that by doing so, they have, in a sense, given in. They have accepted the gang as a fact of life and are being controlled by its values.

Once I started noticing the colour codes that mark out the city's ever-shifting gang boundaries, it was hard to stop. The only alternative to wearing the right colour in a gang-dominated area is to wear something neutral like beige. Many people don the dinge despite the major loss of fashion points (obviously) and any street cred. Given that some Crips-affiliated gangs sometimes wear blue and white for a bit of sartorial variety, even white is risky. Yellow is out too, as some Crips go for the occasional bit of blue and gold. As usual when I am fronting these programmes I wore my continuity black

T-shirts, but as a white man in an almost totally black area I already stuck out like a big sore thumb.

The mayor's office invited me to go out with the St Louis police's dedicated gang unit on patrol. They are doing what they can to stop the killing, end the drugs trade and get the gangs off the street, but with mixed success. Persistently high levels of unemployment still afflict the north St Louis population. The explosive mix of joblessness, fear and the need to belong guarantees a steady stream of recruits to the gangs. Often from homes where one parent is on crack and the other has long since disappeared, too many young kids seek the protection they hope they will get from being part of a pack. When your family is hungry or you feel at risk it can be hard not to make the wrong choice.

In the afternoons you hear the intermittent crackle of fireworks as jobless men sit around in their backyards, drinking the locally brewed Budweiser and Michelob beer and throwing firecrackers at the passing traffic – and now I was around, at me. At first I thought they were just being childish but the facts are more sinister. The background din means that when a real shooting takes place, the explosions delay and sometimes confuse the police. Was that gunfire or just a bunch of good old boys having their usual fun?

One of the very few alternatives to the gangs for young men from deprived areas is the military. Aware of the number of young men desperate for work, US

Marines in immaculate uniforms stalk the city's shopping malls, ushering likely candidates into the signing booths. Some of them end up in Iraq. As a result, competing Bloods and Crips gang graffiti is now turning up on the walls of Baghdad and Fallujah.

Before joining the gang unit on patrol on our third day of filming, I had to change from my usual sandals into trainers in case we ended up in a chase. The only trainers I could get hold of at short notice were bright red. My choice of footwear did not go down at all well. The police and the rest of the crew looked at me askance. Bloods feet. I was in breach of the unwritten colour code.

Travelling slowly and softly in two or more 'low riders' – large unmarked cars – the St Louis PD gang unit operates a lot like the cavalry scouts in the Western movies I watched as a kid. They go looking for signs – only instead of scouring the country for hoofprints they study the buildings and the lamp posts, reading the totems, the graffiti and the tattooed skin of the gangsters themselves for information. What's happening in the neighbourhood? What's the current state of play between the local gangs?

The graffiti the unit showed me looked meaningless at first but a day or two in the expert company of Sergeant Ross and his colleagues taught me how to read it. Every scrawl has its own meaning – a cross through '44 Kitchen Crips', for example, tells you a

Bloods sub-gang is having a problem with the 44s. Called 'X-ing up' or 'X-ing out' the opposition, this kind of tagging means serious trouble. Sometimes an individual opposition gang member is marked with a cross by name. This kind of message boarding gives Ross and the team some idea of where they can next expect trouble and might even mean they get there in time to stop it. Pointing at a new message on a monolithic red-brick wall, Sergeant Ross said, 'This is like reading a newspaper. When we take a look at this, we know the Kitchen Crips are having a problem with the Bloods.'

'Some people get confused because they think the Crips are going to get along with the other Crips. That's not true,' adds one of Ross's colleagues. 'We're not like Los Angeles or Chicago. We're different – it's less neighbourhood here. It's more cross-street. Whenever you see one little gang, their enemies are always nearby. They get into a problem in school or somewhere else and they bring it home here.' Some people say the Bloods and the Crips started life in south Los Angeles, moving east to St Louis along the interstates in the mid-1980s when the LAPD's none-too-gentle crackdown on their activities forced LA gang-bangers to seek their fortunes elsewhere. But whole sectors of Los Angeles are solidly under the influence of either Bloods or the Crips, whereas here in St Louis a lot of sub-gangs will occupy and work a single street.

This aspect of St Louis gang life reminded me

strongly of the way the MS13 gang and its lethal rival 18 Street operate in San Salvador. The gangs are often very small: they occupy very small patches of land and live within shouting distance of their enemies. The proximity of the St Louis neighbourhood gangs guarantees constant tension and violence, just as it does in San Salvador. Operating under the umbrella of the wider gang, sub-gangs, or sets as they sometimes call themselves, adopt all manner of weird and wonderful names: 6 Deuce, Gangster Disciples, JVL Bloods, 44 Kitchen Crips (nothing to do with an interest in cooking and everything to do with the intersection of 44 Street and Kitchen), the Rolling 60s and so on.

I suppose there's always the possibility that, like the tornadoes this city sometimes suffers, the gangs might blow themselves out, but that doesn't look very likely. Official statistics show that more gang-bangers are killed by their supposed allies than by their enemies. Crips kill Crips and Bloods kill Bloods in numbers even greater than they do one another, reinforcing the cycle of violence.

To say the St Louis gangs are permanently at war with one another isn't entirely true. The Crips and the Bloods do sometimes declare a truce. That's when they want to get on with business: drug dealing, burglary, pimping prostitutes, extortion and carjacking.

Since aggressive gang graffiti only serves to ratchet up gang-on-gang violence, when the police have finished deciphering the latest graffiti the authorities send in teams to clean it off. A day or two later the messages promising revenge are usually back. When these threats go up, the gangs mean it: in 2005 the St Louis police recorded eighteen homicides and 280 aggravated assaults in Walnut Park alone, most of them gang-related, making it the city's most dangerous and violent district. One reason for the violence in Walnut Park, I learned, is the close proximity of Interstate 70, which means that users can drive in, score their drugs and be back on the freeway and gone in what for them is a reassuringly short period of time. The huge amounts of money to be made from drugs fuel the relentless war for control of turf, especially lucrative bits like Walnut Park.

Drugs are everywhere in the gang-infested pockets of St Louis – it's impossible to miss the signs of dealing in progress as you drive around. Responding to a call from an unmarked gang unit car ahead, we catch up to find Sergeant Ross's colleagues frisking four black male suspects for drugs and weapons. The baggy blue jeans and white T-shirts say Crips loud and clear. Baseball caps on backwards, the four stand with their hands flat on the boot of their car while the police go through their pockets. Most unit cars carry a laptop in the boot with a wireless connection to police headquarters, meaning officers can take digital photographs of a new suspect and enter these together with names, parents' names, home and mobile telephone numbers and addresses on the unit's extensive database. Then they beam the whole lot to HQ for criminal record checks. They also check the kids for gang tattoos and take snaps of these. In the war against the gangs, information is power.

The area is badly deprived, a ghetto of run-down homes protected by makeshift chicken-wire and chain-link fences, a few people hanging out on their porches watching what's going on. All this name-taking and checking takes a long time. It is a serious annoyance to the kids – not to mention some of the neighbours, who gradually form a small and not very friendly-looking knot across the street. As time goes by and the locals edge closer, I start to feel uncomfortable. Do these kids really deserve all this police attention? They look like the sort of harmless teenagers you might find anywhere. Am I party to the St Louis gang unit flexing its muscles for effect? The suspects certainly seem to think so; it takes all of Sergeant Ross's patience to extract basic information from them; at first they won't even give their names. But just as one suspect is busy protesting there is no arrest warrant out in his name, the routine check comes back: in actual fact two of the four are wanted on outstanding warrants. Ross's men snap on the handcuffs, put the pair in the back of a prowler and take them into custody. The unit count this as a win, if only in that there are two fewer wanted men out on the streets.

The arrested men will get a surprise when they reach

police headquarters: to go with the graphic photographs of gang-on-gang violence that cover the walls of the interrogation suite, the team have stuck up a plain white poster. In the middle of this poster there are two black dots: one is the size of a penny, the other as big as a basketball. Underneath the smaller dot are the words 'Your ass before prison'. Underneath the golf ball-sized dot: 'Your ass when you are in prison'.

Towards the end of my first day on patrol with the gang unit I spot a second bunch of kids out of the corner of my eye. 'What's that?' I ask Ross. The second the kids see the marked patrol car, they start running. Picking up the radio mike Ross shouts right in my ear, 'We've got runners!' He hits the gas, and we are in hot pursuit. The kids are all dressed in blue and white, or blue and gold.

Red trainers pounding in time with my heart, I'm out of the car on the sergeant's heels. The rest of the unit make a fast loop round to the other side of the block to cut off the suspects. Ross and I race through a maze of project housing and low-rise apartments. The scrubby open spaces between are intercut by slatted wooden fences and small alleys, rat runs that might have been made for escape. We are on the tail of about thirteen kids, but they split up and scatter in different directions. We catch up with five, three blokes and two girls all aged between eighteen and twenty. Ross escorts them back to the car, sits them down on the grass verge and the gang team set to work again checking IDs and records. As this is going on Ross tells the grumbling kids, 'We will humiliate and embarrass you every way we can until you give up or go away.' I can tell by the way they are eyeing me the kids think I am with the unit.

'Who are you and what are you doing?' one suddenly blurts. I'm not surprised he wants to know; except for one officer, everyone in the unit is black. As far as I can see I am the only white guy for miles around. More streetwise than the group we caught up with before, these kids are ready with stories. One of the blokes is a walking art gallery: the tattoos on him include the initials LBCG. Ross tells him, 'Long Beach Crips, right? What's the G for?'

The kid has a smart answer: 'Long Beach Community Group.' Shooting him a 'Don't be a wise guy' look, Ross smiles and shakes his head.

The suspect's lady friend has 44 tattooed on her forearm. 'That's how old my momma was when she died,' the girl says.

Ross laughs out loud. 'That's a good one – I gotta write that one down.' The second bloke is wearing an inscription he thinks is witty on his upper arm: 'If it don't make dollars, it don't make cents.' He also has the initials OPAGC. 'What's that mean?' asks Ross.

This one's a joker too; the answer comes back pat: 'O'Fallon Park Area Community Group.'

Another unit member leans to inspect the letters and says drily, 'Or it could say O'Fallon Park Associated

Gangster Crips.' The kid shakes his head; he says the police are confusing him.

When Ross gently points out that sporting Crips colours in this area puts him at clear and present risk of death by shooting, and he might want to think about wearing something a bit more neutral, the suspect blurts, 'This is my life. I'm in a culture. I don't shoot people – I've been shot three times. My own brother got killed in these streets; my grandmother lives right there, man. Brothers, please don't get me confused. Because I'm going to stay true to what I believe in. And I believe in it.'

Gang unit policy is to get in the face of the gangsters and make them understand who controls the streets, but is it working? Not if this attitude is anything to go by. When I put this to Sergeant Ross, he didn't agree: 'It's a worthy cause. Whether we get one person or a hundred people out, it's a worthy cause. This [the gang unit] is something that's needed in this city and a lot of cities. What's going on here in St Louis is going on everywhere.'

As well as reading gang signs and trying to make life uncomfortable for gangsters, Ross and his team spend a lot of their time searching for weapons in the stinking, filthy debris of the many abandoned buildings. I really didn't like going into those rat-infested holes – long-abandoned basements filled with rotting rubbish, crumbling outbuildings and dark, mouldy rooms – but it needs doing. In fact it is a very important part of the unit's job. Rather than get arrested for possession of an illegal firearm, which can earn you up to ten years in jail, many gang-bangers keep caches of weapons in handy locations all over their home turf. Ross's partner said, 'It's called a community weapon – everybody on the block knows where it is. If they need it, they'll get it, use it and put it back.'

The most common method of initiating a wannabe member into the Bloods or Crips is to get him to walk into a rival gang's territory and shoot it up. If he comes back out in one piece, the guy is in. Another initiation ceremony, very like one used by the MS13 and 18 Street gangs in El Salvador, is known as beating in. The gang forms a circle or two lines, and the would-be member gets a kicking in the middle. If he stands up to it well and earns the gang's respect, then he's in. Both rites give the gang some idea of whether the new kid has got what it takes, but with this level of violence more and more citizens like Arthella Spence are voting with their feet, negating the influx of immigrants. As people move out of the city, schools close down, forcing children from one neighbourhood to travel to another. This causes more gang warfare because it dumps groups of kids from Bloods-controlled parts of town in among their Crips rivals and vice versa. Disputes that start as childish disagreements in the schoolyard often end up being resolved on the streets. In far too many cases 'resolved' means the argument ends up in violence and sometimes death. Up until a few years ago small-scale, essentially unimportant disputes of this kind would have been settled with fists, as they were in my school. Now, many of the schoolkids have guns and are prepared to use them.

The biggest current teenage flashpoint in the city is a local school on Cass Avenue, an example of ill-advised – or wildly optimistic – planning if ever there was one. The new air-conditioned school was supported by lots of local businesses and private institutions, hoping that its $47.3 million-worth of shining new architecture would be the catalyst for change the area so needs. It is a beautiful building, with media centre, swimming pool and competition-standard gyms. But this school lies bang in the middle of territory claimed both by the JVL (Jefferson Van der Loo) Bloods and their deadly rivals, the 26-MAD Crips.

Since it opened in 2002 the area around the school has seen regular violent battles between the two main gangs. According to the gang unit, even during vacation time, when it is closed, kids from warring gangs hang around outside the school looking for trouble. When Ross and his colleagues stop to warn them they are likely to end up in the city morgue, most just shrug their shoulders. 'At that age,' he says, 'they believe they are invincible. But a bullet doesn't care how old or young you are.'

As we drove around I kept seeing groups of younger

children performing all kinds of amazing gymnastics: back flips and front flips and vaults on mattresses dragged out of empty houses and laid on the grass by the side of the road. There is so little else for them to do and so much obvious athletic talent going to waste. But unless things change a lot of them will inevitably drift into the gangs.

One organization trying to help the city's youth get out of the gangs or stop them joining in the first place is the Brothers of Islam. Led by a large charismatic man named Kabir Mohammed, the Brothers of Islam hold gang-avoidance workshops once a week in a local school. *Kabir* means big in Arabic, and Mohammed is big, both physically and as a personality. An ex-member who lost a brother to gang violence, he is not one to mince words when it comes to telling it like it is about the realities of gang life. Faced with fifty or so kids either already in gangs or at risk of getting sucked in, what Kabir tells them is all the more powerful for being based on his own experience. When someone in the audience objects that the way he is speaking to them shows disrespect, Kabir loses it: 'Fuck you! I'm trying to save your lives, man! I got people out there want to kill me for what I do. And damn, we got society feeding you with all this so fucked-up music, all these fucked-up videos. So no – I ain't changing shit. This is how it's going to be; this is how we get down. Straight, right to the fucking point. Now, goddamnit, you can accept the truth and live, or you can reject it and fucking die.'

As he tells it, the white people who control the music and video industry manipulate many black musicians into broadcasting messages of violence, misogyny and general hatred, not to mention the use and sale of drugs. Encouraging black-on-black gang violence in this way is, he insists, 'the white man's way of keeping the black man down'. The words seem to strike home. Listening and watching, even I am a bit scared. Kabir's shouted delivery is brutal, but it needs to be. Looking at the hardened faces of the kids, I don't think a softly-softly, 'Wouldn't it be nice if we talked through our problems' approach is going to cut much ice.

Kabir doesn't try to pretend there is any easy way out of the car crash waiting to happen that is life for so many young north St Louis kids. Given the difficulty of reaching them and how little respect they have for authority, the fact that he gets any of them to come and hear him speak at all is little short of a miracle. Some come because other gang-bangers have told them about the Brothers of Islam, and this alone is a sign he is reaching them. But Kabir also goes out on the streets in person, finds these kids and encourages them to come along.

He moves on to take a swipe at the way he believes some big-name US companies are ready to exploit gang culture for profit. 'Is the chairman of Nike a black man? Of course not – he's a white man.' He also points out that some businesses are making money on the back of gang culture. St Louis sports shops, he tells me, divide their merchandise according to gang colours: Bloods red on one side, Crips blue and white on the other. I went to see for myself. Many of them do.

All really young, the boys sit there on the hard wood chairs, and they listen and watch Big Mohammed do his stuff. I could tell he scared them just a little. But two things about the meeting worried me: when I looked around the room, most of the kids were still wearing red or blue, and when I visited the toilet, there on the walls was more gang graffiti. One scrawl, written in pencil above the sink taps had an arrow pointing at the soap and read, 'Crips don't use this.' The insult may be childish, but it tells you everything about the mindset.

Kabir asks a fifteen-year-old in the group why young people his age 'get involved in gangs even knowing it can cost you your life'. He gets an equally direct response. 'People join gangs so they get to feel like they belong to something. If your family messed up and stuff, your momma on crack and stuff, it makes you feel like you belong to someone, like you want to be somewhere.' Hard to argue with that one.

The guy sitting next to him pipes up, 'I was born on the East Side.'

'Gangster Disciples?' Kabir asks.

The kid nods. 'My uncle got killed over there, in his apartment.'

'Was he a gang member?'

'Yeah. He was going downstairs. Dudes came, and they shot him on the ground. I was in my room and they were shooting at my window. A bullet came in through my window. That's when I saw him on the ground. Blood was all on the ground. They told me to go back in my room.'

'How old were you then?'

'I was seven.'

I asked the first kid, 'What age were you when you first knew there were drugs in your neighbourhood?'

He said, 'My grandmother told me this story about when I was little and I used to come over her house. It was December, and the cold was real bad and there was snow on the ground in the street. And I fell in the snow and I picked it up and I said, "I'm going to eat this stuff." And when she saw me wanting to eat snow, that's when my grandmother realized my momma was on crack.'

You can see why Kabir struggles to make the kids understand that the gangs are the problem, not the solution to their smashed-up lives.

Do I think Kabir Mohammed is doing a great job? Without question. Do I think he has an uphill struggle? All the way. Will he ever make a significant lasting difference to the gang-ridden streets of north St Louis? Even with the help of Islam and its powerful message of living a drug- and alcohol-free life, I'm not convinced. But if he saves even one kid from the gangs, as

Sergeant Ross says, Kabir Mohammed's almighty effort has to be worth it.

I'd been in the city of St Louis for a week and felt as if I hadn't met any of the 'real' gangsters who wreak havoc in their communities, the kind who kill the Robert Walkers of this world and bequeath their families decades of grief. And then I met one.

Jason Hampton was not only a gangster but one of the biggest men I have ever met. At about six feet six inches and 280 pounds, twenty-six-year-old Hampton would not have looked out of place playing for the St Louis Rams. A former JVL Blood, I got to know him through the local parole board. (Jason was out after several years behind bars for drugs trafficking and illegal possession of a firearm.) Hampton's parole officer, Carol, looked all of fifteen years old. In fact, she's in her twenties and carries a Glock 9mm. I am not sure whether Carol's sidearm encouraged Jason to stick to the terms of his parole, but it definitely sets her apart from her British counterparts.

A long-term Blood, Jason saw the light when a rival gang member crept up on him, clapped a pistol to the back of his head and pulled the trigger. The round failed to explode, perhaps because the cordite inside was past its sell-by date, but for Jason his escape was a life-changing incident. As he told me, 'This stuff ain't no game. If someone come up and puts a gun to your head and pulls the trigger and that gun don't go off, that's a sign. You know what I'm saying? A sign you gotta wake up, brother.'

He took me on a guided tour of the mean scabby streets he had grown up on and fought over before his arrest and imprisonment. Stopping in front of a dilapidated clapboard house, Jason pointed to the bullet holes that peppered its façade. Then, turning to look across the street, he said, 'This here is Bloods turf; right over there is the Crips. Come night time, they get in the mood, they come right on over, shoot first and ask later.' The opposition didn't need to drive by – they could just walk across the street and start blazing away. He said it was mostly about drugs. All types dropped by to score. 'Folks was coming from everywhere. We have people coming from St Charles, we had guys coming from Springfield, truck drivers stopping, picking up hookers, the hookers bringing them over here. My first day at high school, I had $800 in my pocket.'

When I started secondary school at the age of eleven I was lucky if I had a couple of quid. I stared at Hampton to see if he was telling the truth. 'Eight hundred dollars?'

'Eight hundred dollars. Jewellery on, everything. It was just how you get money, and that's what we was doing, we was just getting money.'

He talked me through some of the gang graffiti sprayed on the pavement. 'Velar, that's the homeboy who got killed in a high-speed chase with the police. BIP stands for Blood in Peace. 31 Tray ACE. Thirty-one is the block right here.' He pointed at the area behind him.

In the daytime Jason said the streets were usually quiet; the gang-bangers were sleeping. It was night when most of the dealing and the killing and the robbing took place. He stopped at an intersection and nodded at the street opposite. Even in broad daylight he did not dare drive down it. When I asked him why, he shrugged. 'I can't go there. If I do, they'll kill me.' This was a grown man, one of the biggest I had ever met, a larger-than-life character like someone out of a Raymond Chandler novel. And yet he was afraid to leave his own neighbourhood. He said he never stopped at traffic lights, he rolled through them at a slow, steady speed ready to step on the gas if killers came running up to shoot him where he sat. It's a favourite St Louis gang execution method.

As we drove, I thought that although Jason was out on parole, where it counted he was still in prison: confined to his own little patch in fear of his life. In the land of the free, Jason Hampton had no freedom. As he said himself, this is no way for a grown-up to live. 'There's no life in these gangs, so you just got to leave it alone. Sometimes you just got to look at yourself and ask: Is this what you want? Is this how you're going to settle for your kids as they get older? I'm tired of seeing my partners, my friends and my associates all going to jail. Either there or dead – it hurts. It's just time to wise up, man, leave this gang stuff alone.' Amen to that. I left Jason Hampton on the porch at his home, trying to wade back to dry land from the gang swamp. All we can do is wish him luck.

Hampton had taken me closer to the front line, but he was a reformed gangster. It didn't seem right to leave St Louis without meeting some active, hard-core gang members if I could. It was a big if. Making contact with seriously bad guys isn't just difficult, it's like herding cats. The way it worked? Our local fixer knew someone who knew someone else who had agreed to talk. After four hours waiting in a hot stuffy car in a wind-blown parking lot being taken for undercover cops by local dealers, I decided it wasn't going to happen. I'd had enough; we'd have to give it a miss and go home. But then, as we started to pull out of the parking lot, the phone call came through.

Waiting for gangsters in the heat for hours on end is bad for the nerves, but fear lends its own edge, one I found quite useful as we followed our contact out to meet the leading Blood who had agreed to an interview. We eventually pulled up outside a tumbledown house at the end of an unpaved track in a low-rent district. Here, the few homes looked long-abandoned. Bits of junk loomed up out of the darkness as I approached the house. I had no idea where we were but I knew one thing for sure: I did not like the look of this place one little bit. I liked it even less when I tripped on a low mound of earth and fell. I didn't realize it at the time, but I had fallen over the grave of a dog. I ignored the loud knocking sound coming from the inside of my ribcage and pushed in through the open front door. Nobody else knew we were here; we were totally in their hands.

Inside, the house was poorly lit. There was no one there. At first I thought we'd been set up. Then two older men appeared. They looked exhausted and emaciated, like classic crack addicts. They told me the big man would be coming later. One produced a thin piece of brass piping about the length of a biro. One end of it was sealed with plumber's tape. He took a bag out and stuck a rock of crack into the open end of the tube, pushed it down with a metal nail, flicked a cigarette lighter and heated the pipe. As I waited in the gloom, the acrid smell of burning crack filled the room. The other guy was smoking a More brand cigarette, except it seemed to be having a much bigger effect on him than usual.

These guys told me the Bloods paid them in drugs to work on houses being done up as part of a city-wide regeneration project. It was one way they had of laundering money. Even better, this type of project sometimes attracted municipal funding, increasing the profits. Looking at the standard of their work and the amount of narcotics they were getting through, I won't be asking this pair to come round and retile my bathroom.

A young bloke with a white T-shirt over his face suddenly walked in. The way he had it arranged made him look like a Tuareg tribesman. Even though he was obviously very young, the older guys clearly respected him, stepping back out of his way. The kid beckoned me out. I followed him through a dank room, empty except for a couple of plastic garden chairs along a corridor, and out into a second, larger room at the back of the house. The smell of dog excrement grew stronger and stronger, and then a loud chorus of barking broke out in the night. There were pit bulls out in the backyard locked up in metal cages. 'Turn off the camera light,' the kid told us; he was worried it might attract the police or rival gangsters.

I was just trying to get my bearings when a second man loomed up out of the darkness. This guy was very big. Really scary, wearing a frightening plastic mask. Like a cross between an African tribal mask and an ice hockey goalkeeper's, it was a long white oval that covered his whole face except for the mouth. Dark, angry eyes gleamed through elongated slits that curled up and back in a teardrop shape. There was a strange green stylized cross painted in the top centre of the mask while the rest of it was striped with a red geometric design. He wore heavy-duty gardening gloves, and he was carrying the corpse of a dead American pit bull puppy in one hand and a red Bloods bandanna in the other. He looked both sinister and surreal, a figure from a horror movie involving chainsaws.

In a deep, slurring voice that sounded as if it had been slowed down mechanically to half-speed and then scrambled, the big, shambling figure said something about burying another dog the previous day. Wrapping its tiny body in the Bloods bandanna, he scooped a shallow grave in the loose dirt of the backyard, placed the dog inside and then covered it up. The ceremony complete, he turned and led me back inside to the room with the plastic chairs. The young bloke turned up again and ordered the older guys to 'shut the fuck up'. We moved upstairs. Mask Man and his young apprentice sat down on a battered old sofa. I pulled over a white plastic chair and sat down opposite on the edge of the seat.

Leaning forward, I asked Mask Man how he had first become a gang member. As he rolled and lit a spliff he said, 'Grew up all our life on the set, that's what's up.' (By 'set' he meant a gang-dominated neighbourhood.)

I asked, 'Was there pressure on you?'

As if things weren't already bizarre enough, great clouds of smoke from the newly lit spliff billowed out from his mask, making it even harder to see him in the half light than before. 'Never no pressure. The streets, that's what's it. Streets ain't gonna feed ya shit.'

As my eyes grew more accustomed to the gloom I could make out bin bags filled with different types of marijuana on the floor in front of me, and small clear screw-top bottles like urine sample jars filled with a light yellow liquid. Mask Man called this water. I picked one of the bottles up, cracked the top and smelled its contents. 'Smells like paint thinner. What is it?'

Taking the filter out of a cigarette and 'loosening the square' – shaking out some of the tobacco inside so that it soaked up some of the 'water' – he showed me why the man downstairs had relished his smoke. 'Water is PCP, man. They loving it all the time for twenty bucks.'

PCP stands for phenylcyclohexylpiperidine. It induces dissociative anaesthesia – users know they are being touched, undergoing pain or having some other sensory experience but they can't actually feel anything. Trialled by US surgical units in the 1960s, it was withdrawn after patients reported all kinds of terrible symptoms: feeling as if they had died, delirium, terrifying hallucinations, out-of-body experiences and slurred and scrambled speech. In its crystalline form PCP is often known as angel dust. In its liquid form I had just found out it is sometimes called water.

'What about crack?' I wanted to know. Mask Man reached down, undid his flies and started rummaging about in his crotch. This wasn't quite the answer I had been expecting, but his underpants had more space inside them than the Tardis. I couldn't believe the amount of drugs he pulled out of there, plucking out little packets and bags like Santa Claus pulling presents from his sack. One by one, very slowly and carefully, he laid them out like trophies on the floor in front of me.

I asked Mask Man how he protected his turf. Reaching down into the cavernous underpants for a second time, he pulled out what he called 'my nine' (9 millimetre), in actual fact a Colt .45 pistol. Working the slide and chambering a round, he cocked the hammer. 'There's one in there,' he slurred in case I hadn't noticed. Great – I was now sitting six feet from a very stoned gang leader with the hammer back on a pistol that leaves an exit wound in your back the size of a plate.

Mask Man delved down into the vast and roomy reaches of his underpants yet again and this time drew out a round block of brown heroin about the size and thickness of a pub ashtray. I couldn't help wondering how it had managed to make the journey from the fields of Afghanistan to the back lots of St Louis and down into his pants. Catching my eye, he offered to sell me the entire lump for $75,000. I'm no expert, but I suspect this was a real bargain.

His sidekick, who had been quiet until now, suddenly piped up, 'Your nine's your best friend, man.' By way of agreement, Mask Man kissed the Colt, and then just to make himself look even weirder put a red Bloods bandanna over his head.

As he kissed the pistol I wondered out loud, 'Have you ever used it?'

With the hammer still back and the gun pointing directly at me, Mask Man said slowly, 'This one got served to some players. They was playing a game, but they got played. But this is just a little toy.'

'You have bigger toys?'

'Yeeuh,' he said in his thick Missouri accent. 'Those

big toys, they shoot lots of times.' Waving the pistol in a way that was seriously scary, he turned to his young mate. 'How do you use that?'

'Bang, bang, bang, bang,' said his buddy in a bored tone.

The weed was making Mask Man paranoid. 'Spend time smoking weed . . . I'm nervous.'

Not as nervous as I am, I thought, as he laid the pistol on the ground, still with the hammer back and still pointing my way. Clearly Mask Man was a major dealer. There was so much stuff he seemed to have forgotten where some of it was hidden and began upending buckets of dog biscuits and animal litter to find it. I suspected the paper-thin cover for his dealing was the dog kennels downstairs. In the event of a bust you have to have a way of explaining your income – and the dogs would also help keep unwanted visitors at bay. Scrabbling in a bucket filled with dog pellets, he took out a big bag of weed and offered to sell it to me at a 'special friend discount'. I thanked him and politely declined.

What with his paranoia and my own concerns about ending up with the puppies under a mound outside, I decided it was time to call it a night. Hoping I hadn't offended him by not wishing to take a kilo of marijuana or some heroin back to the hotel with me, I got up to go. Before I left, he showed me how to do a Bloods handshake. The proverb warns, 'Be careful of what you wish for; it may come true.' I'd got what I'd wished for

– I'd met the real deal, and the real deal was very, very scary.

It was time to say goodbye to St Louis. Echoing in my ears was the last thing Jason Hampton had told me: 'There's a war going on across the seas, but there's a war going on in the United States every day.' Having seen what I'd seen in his home city, I was inclined to agree with him.

5. Cape Town

Pollsmoor prison is an assault on the senses. What hits you first is the smell – a mix of fear, sweat and dirt, the hot, all-pervasive smell of one of South Africa's most notorious maximum-security prisons. Then there's the noise – the background roar of thousands of caged men, cut through with shouts and screams.

Pollsmoor sits in an otherwise pleasant area of countryside some twenty-five kilometres from Cape Town. The road winds through a patchwork of vineyards, market gardens, upmarket housing and attractive open land. From a distance, you could be forgiven for mistaking the place for a large, horribly designed 1960s comprehensive school. Oddly, right next to it is a lush private golf course. But the closer you get, the worse Pollsmoor looks: a grim series of gaunt, three- and four-storey blocks pierced with rows of small, heavily barred windows, it shows a blank and forbidding face to the world. To make their time inside that bit crueller, none of the prisoners' windows faces out towards freedom and the light.

Lulled by the sunshine drive through some of the Cape's spectacularly beautiful scenery, now I'd arrived the reality of Pollsmoor hit home all the harder. Most visitors to the area were living it up, abseiling off Table Mountain, hiking up through the Tokai Forest to Elephant's Eye cave or doing some wine tasting at the Steenberg Vineyards, Africa's oldest wine estate a mile or so away. Famous for its inhumanity, Pollsmoor was a bit of a short straw. The prison is where Nelson Mandela spent the last four years of his time inside and where he caught the tuberculosis that nearly killed him.

I was in Pollsmoor to find out what I could about South Africa's most notorious and deadly gang, the Number or Numbers gang. The Number is one of the world's most secretive and strange gangs, unique in that it exists only in South Africa's prisons, above all in the prison we were now entering. In reality five associated jails, Pollsmoor is spread over a huge site. On any given day more than 7,000 prisoners are banged up inside, more than twice the number it was originally built to hold back in 1964.

Senior Warder Chris Malgas, who escorted me into the prison, was my guide for the duration. He told me that the ratio of guards to prisoners is roughly 1:100. I stared at him. One guard to oversee every hundred of the world's most volatile and dangerous prisoners? With such a dangerously low ratio of guards to guarded, the warders in Pollsmoor don't even carry guns – the risk of inmates snatching them is too great. Unarmed, more than half the warders at any one time have been stabbed. One of the guards recently had his eye cut out; soon after that a gangster stabbed a trainee warder to death. There are no white warders or staff inside the prison proper – they are all either black or Cape Coloured.

As we followed the new arrivals in through the stringent security, the short hairs on the back of my neck began to rise. I felt a creeping sense of violence that increased with every step.

Malgas is an easy-going rugby fanatic. Like many of the guards, he lives on site with his family. In his quiet, contained manner he explained that all visitors, like all prisoners, are searched – if not quite in the same way. The warders are looking mainly for alcohol, knives, drugs and other prohibited items; the other day, Malgas said, a tennis ball full of drugs had been thrown over the wall. As the sniffer dogs did their work, he said that even for a prisoner being held overnight the chances of being beaten and raped by the Number are better than one in two. Not odds I would personally take.

'There are three divisions of the Number gang,' he said, 'the 28s, the 27s and the 26s. The 28s are the foot soldiers. They are creatures of the night, interested in power. The 27s are the assassins – they kill the enemies of the Number not just here in Pollsmoor but in every South African prison. Every time they kill for the gang, the 27 assassins have more time added to their sentences. This means they live and die in prison.'

'And the 26s?'

'The 26s do fight, but they care more about money than power. They make income for the 27s and the

28s. They are confidence tricksters.' He gestured at the milling prisoners. 'You can tell the Number by their chappies.'

'Chappies?'

'Their tattoos. They cut them in with a razor blade and then rub black Bic biro ink in the wound.' I saw that the men divided into those with tattoos covering their faces and their bodies, and those who had none.

By now we were in the squalid admissions yard. The guards made the new arrivals line up and strip naked. Then one after another they came forward, squatted on their haunches and bounced up and down. The warders scanned the ground beneath the bouncing men with an eagle eye. The sight was shocking and very humiliating. 'Why are they making them do that?'

'They are looking for the poke,' Malgas said.

'The poke?'

'A plastic tube they insert in their anus. It holds things the Number gangsters inside the prison want – mostly drugs, weapons or money. It can also be something like a SIM card for a mobile phone. Often, these are items that have been ordered by a senior Number.'

'Why would anyone want to stick a plastic tube up their backside and risk getting caught smuggling?'

'On their way into prison the Number gangsters who are with a new batch of men approach those who are not in the gang. They tell them, "You will take this poke into the prison."'

'Where do they do this? In the prison van?'

'In the van or sometimes in a police cell even before that.' I glanced back at the guys doing the weird squat routine in the yard. 'What happens if the guy won't take the poke?'

'If a man refuses . . .' Malgas paused.

'What?'

'The Number tell him they will cut out his eye.' He gave a grim nod. 'Sometimes they do it – so the others will obey.'

'So you either have a poke up your backside with drugs or whatever in it or the Number gangsters cut your eye out?'

'Yes.'

'What happens if the man accepts the poke?'

'If he accepts the poke, then his troubles have begun.'

'How?'

'The Number claim him as a *wyfie*.' A completely new word to me, Malgas pronounced it with a strong Afrikaans accent: 'vyfie'. You didn't have to be a genius to guess what it might mean but I asked anyway: 'What's a *wyfie*?'

'A *wyfie* is a slave to the Number. The 28s use violence and sodomy to dominate the new inmates. A *wyfie* has to give the Number man who owns him sex when he wants it. He has to wash the Number's clothes, cook his food, clean for him and do everything his Number master tells him to do.'

'And if he doesn't? If he tries to resist?'

Malgas shrugged. 'If he tries to resist they will either beat him to say yes or they will kill him. A 27 assassin comes to kill him on the orders of the 28s.' This sounded to me like a good reason for obeying, but at the same time part of me didn't really want to believe what this man was telling me. Slavery might have been officially abolished in most countries, but if what Malgas told me was true, right here in Pollsmoor it was flourishing.

'How many people say yes to the poke?'

'Who can tell? But we find many while they are doing this.' He gestured at the parade of men in the yard undergoing the humiliating ritual.

'What happens if he gets the stuff inside the prison? Do the Number reward him or let him join the gang?'

Malgas was a kind and good-natured man. He didn't laugh at my questions, only smiled. 'If he does succeed in smuggling something in the poke, the new man is told, "Take what you have to Mr X on so-and-so wing, and he will look after you."'

I could tell by the way he said 'look after you' that there was more to it than he was telling me. And it was bad. 'How do you mean, "look after"?'

'Sometimes the poke gets stuck inside the smuggler. To get it out, they hold him down and one of the Number hooks it out with a wire coat hanger.' I stared at Malgas. All of this was horrible – about as bad as it could get – and it was happening in one of South Africa's official state institutions.

I looked at the men in the yard with a new eye. Most looked terrified. No wonder: those not in the gang knew that from this moment on they were at the mercy of the Number – vulnerable to serial rape, beatings, robbery, enslavement and murder. As we watched the new men shuffle over to the desks for registration and their issue of bright orange prison clothing, I saw the knowledge of what they faced in their pinched, desperate looks. They wanted help. And they wanted out of there. I felt especially for the younger guys, the teenagers, who were in the majority. But I knew that for them there was no escape.

Nearly all of the prisoners in Pollsmoor describe themselves as Cape Coloured – mixed-race people who live mainly in the townships on the Cape Flats, a barren tract of land to the east of Table Mountain. This was where the apartheid regime had dumped many workers it evicted from their homes in the 1960s under race laws. Now, together with thousands of new immigrants, they make up nearly half Cape Town's population.

Malgas told me that the Number call any prisoner not one of their own a *frans*, a word that means something like worthless or subhuman. As with the Nazis, this kind of labelling helps one group of humans persecute another. A *frans* either agrees to serve the Number as a *wyfie* or he fights. If he fights, and by some miracle of strength, speed and luck survives the ordeal, the Number might invite him to join one of their gangs.

If he loses, he is a dead man walking. It is the most extreme example of survival of the fittest I have ever come across.

Forced anal and oral sex? Enslavement? Serving some Number gangster as a kind of abject domestic servant? Judging by what I had found out about the gang so far, part of me thought death was a better option than ending up as a Number's *wyfie*.

What would you do?

There was plenty more. *Wyfies* have to sit silent and facing the cell wall when the Number are present; they have to do what Number gangsters want instantly and without question, even down to cutting their toenails; and if a *wyfie* gets a parcel from a relative or friend, the Number grab the goodies. It is as if the world's most extreme misogynists are acting out some ultra-violent, ultra-oppressive fantasy, only the victims are men, not women.

One of the biggest surprises was the military-style rank badges etched into the faces and bodies of the tattooed men I could see around me in the yard. They were very like the ones the British army uses, and included stripes on the arms for corporals and sergeants and crudely tattooed shoulder stars like pips for officers. There was something old fashioned about these tattooed insignia, as if they had been copied from British uniforms of about the time of the nineteenth-century Zulu Wars.

Spotting a man with four tattooed pips on each

shoulder, which suggested he was a senior officer in the Number, I walked up to him. The prisoner was probably in his thirties, but the squashed, dissolving facial features that are the telltale result of crystal methamphetamine abuse made him look much older. Not a big man, the convict had a knotty physique and a blank, dead expression in his eyes that made him very, very scary to be near. 'I Dig My Grave Evil One' and 'I Cry for Blood' competed for space with dozens of other chappies and the scars of knife and bullet wounds on his face and upper body. Many Number gangsters cut a star-shaped tattoo into their forearms every time they kill someone; there were so many stars on his arms there was hardly any bare skin left. A large tattoo covered his back showing a man being raped – not the kind of thing you would expect to find on offer in your local tattoo parlour.

I asked which of the three Number divisions he belonged to. It took him some time to reply. When he did it was like listening to a man speaking from the bottom of a deep well; there was a strangeness in him. 'The 28s.'

'How long have you been in the 28s?'

'Twenty-eight years,' he replied without irony. 'I am a senior officer.'

'Which branch of the 28s?'

'The blood line.' The blood line is the fighting wing of the 28s.

A younger man standing nearby suddenly butted in:

Ciudad Barrios – attempting to keep your whites whiter than white

Making the MS sign

Failed removal of a tattoo

Tributes to the dead in St Louis: sad statements of loss involving the very young to gang violence

A short life

In your face policing from the gang unit

Mask Man, the Blood gang leader (*right*), and his young apprentice

Pollsmoor prison, Cape Town

Being made to squat while officers check for the poke

John Mongrel, the scariest man I've ever met . . . so far

Me with the high-ranking 26s and a *wyfie* in the background

Having a conversation with kids in the Cape Flats

Dimitri in full Nazi flow

Practising for the duel

Me on fire

Wani with Martin

Me and Fast Mover's bodyguard

Gangsters in the Grants Pen garrison with Donovan looking on

'Don't speak to the camera.' The 28 shrugged and turned away.

'He won't speak more,' Malgas said. 'It is the Number code. Anyone who tells the gang's secrets is killed.'

It was time to go up to the second floor of the super-maximum security wing that housed some of the most dangerous Number gang members. Two cells had agreed to be interviewed; whether they would talk openly about the gang was another matter. I glanced at Malgas, then stopped and looked at him harder. There was a concerned expression on his face I hadn't seen till now. He was feeling the fear. If he was a little worried then, I should be very worried.

'You will see some beds are curtained off; these are the bunks of the officers and their *wyfies*. You will find it is dark in the cells. We had to put metal sheets over the windows after the neighbours outside the prison complained about the noise. Remember: you focus; you keep a soft face; you breathe, you make eye contact and you think. You never show them any fear. The Number are pack animals: if you show them fear, they are on top of you.' I took him to mean that literally.

I thought the advice about the 'soft face' was interesting. Malgas kept his face expressionless almost all of the time. I suppose if you don't give any emotion out then the prisoners can't pick up on it.

Inside the prison it was stark and surprisingly cold: the thick stone walls kept the intense summer heat outside. I could see why Nelson Mandela might have fallen ill. We walked along a bare grey corridor towards the first of the big group cells. Out of nowhere a bright wink of light caught my eye. It was a reflection from a scrap of shaving mirror taped to the end of a stick projecting from between the bars of a cell up ahead. Then more mirrors on sticks began to appear, like the antennae of some strange insect. Most were car wing mirrors: the gangsters wanted to see who was coming. Forewarned being forearmed, in Pollsmoor mirrors are high on the list of prized possessions.

Malgas unlocked the door of the first cell and we stepped inside. It was dark, as he had warned me it would be, so dark that for a moment, coming in from the brightness outside, it took time for your eyes to adjust. I tried to leave a part of my brain – the bit with the fear in it – outside in the corridor. If I had thought the smell in the rest of the prison was bad, in here it was raw: a thick, soupy, caged-animal stink so thick you could chew it. Except for the warders, hardly anyone but the prisoners themselves ever goes inside these cells. Two- and three-tier bunk beds lined the walls. Men stood staring at us in knots of three or four. Meeting their gaze, it was hard not to feel intimidated. We were now totally under their control; I just had to hope that Malgas would keep us safe.

Remembering what Malgas had said, I tried my hardest to relax and show none of the fear I was feeling. As a way of controlling it, I tried to focus on details. I noticed that a lot of the prisoners were missing their front teeth – not as the result of fights but because in Pollsmoor having a gaping hole where they used to be is the height of fashion. If they can afford it, prisoners have gold substitutes put in. Most inmates just have the gap.

This was the hard core of the Number gang, men who had nothing to lose. The worst thing that could happen to them was to get more time in Pollsmoor, but many of them were serving life sentences anyway.

Hardly daring to look round, *wyfies* sat on the lower bunks, silent. Three leaders of the 28s came forward. They were very interested in the sound equipment we had with us – not for the kit itself but for the batteries, which can be used to power things like mobile phones. As with mirrors, batteries are one of Pollsmoor's most valuable currencies. They made gang recognition signals with their fingers and hands.

At first no one would say much. I was finding it pretty hard to understand them anyway. South Africa has eleven official languages, but most people from the Cape Flats speak Kapie-taal, a mix of Afrikaans with English and Xhosa, a mainly southern language. Add to that the special dialects used by the gangs, Tsotsi-taal and Fly-taal, and as an English-only outsider you are in trouble. The boys have some pretty pithy ways of wishing you dead: *Ek sal jou witbiene maak*, for instance – 'I'll turn you into white bones.' Quite a few of the prisoners did not speak any English at all. Those who did had a strong, guttural accent mixed with lots of attitude.

When I made it clear I did not expect them to tell me the inner secrets of the gang and just wanted to talk about the kind of things that happened inside Pollsmoor some of the guys in the cell began to loosen up. The weird thing was that, as bad as they looked and as hard as they were, some of them were giggling and nudging one another like schoolboys. They would stab you as soon as look at you, but there was a strange childlike side to them. Perhaps it came from spending so much of their lives in an institution.

But there the comparison with kids ends. They told me what they usually do when a new prisoner decides to fight rather than give in and become a *wyfie*. It immediately became clear we were not talking about a fair contest. Surrounding their prey, the gang set about him with a range of weapons. Made out of what comes to hand, these include metal prison mugs fastened to leather belts. To make it more deadly, the rim of the mug is sharpened to a cutting edge. They also use heavy metal padlocks tied to belts or lengths of nylon strap. The victim has little chance. Surrounding him, five or six of the Number attack at a signal. 'You have to do it with this side,' said a man holding a mug on the end of a belt. He turned the mug in his hand and ran a fingertip around the sharpened rim. It made me shudder just to look at it. That was going to slice a man's scalp wide.

'Why that side?' I asked.

'So you make the blood come open.'

A second 28 handed me one of the padlock weapons. 'Feel the weight and see what it can do to a person's skull,' he said. I weighed the thing in my hand and gave the padlock an experimental swing. Your basic low-tech implement, there was no doubt at all it could kill. 'The heavier the lock the better,' said this expert at hurting people. 'If you crack his skull, you've got him.' He took the strap back. 'You must not take it long like this,' he said in a heavy voice, 'because I can catch this thing. Then I cut you.' Grabbing hold of it right up close to the lock so that it was an extension of his fist, he demonstrated, thwacking the weapon into his palm in a series of flat, vicious blows. 'You must keep it shorter, like this.' I had another go, and this time the approving murmur of the men in the cell told me I had done it right.

Always nice to learn new skills.

Aiming for the skull, where it not only hurts the most but stands to do the greatest damage, the gangsters bash anyone who dares stand up to them until he either dies or does what they want. Sometimes, as if massed padlocks weren't enough, an attacker armed with a knife will stand off a little from the main assault group. One of the 28s in the second cell we now went into showed me how he did it. 'I step in when I see him and I take shots.' He stabbed with an imaginary knife, holding it horizontal and jabbing with fast, short-armed, vicious thrusts. In Pollsmoor speak, 'taking shots' means stabbing. The biggest problem for the person on the end of all this is that he has no idea when the Number will stop beating and stabbing him. Or even stop at all.

The gangsters told me the same treatment is handed out to anyone who crosses the Number or breaches gang rules, especially its code of silence. But when they come after you for a transgression, the Number don't bother with tin mugs – it's the heavy metal padlock. And they stab you for real. The pale scars and laceration marks on their heads and bodies made it clear the men standing around me had all been through the mill.

Even if a man survives a Number beating, there is another test of his mettle before he can join the gang: he must stab a warder or another prisoner to order. One or more of the senior 28s chooses the target. I got lucky: one of the men I was talking to told me how it had happened with him. 'They told me I could join, but first I had to stab a man. Not a prisoner, one of the warders. When I asked them how, they said I would get a knife, and as soon as it came I had to go and find Mr Murray and kill him.'

'Did you do it?'

'I didn't believe they would get me a knife in the prison. But the next day a Number came and put one in my hand. He was passing. Straight away I covered it and hid it. Followed by other 28s, I found Mr Murray. The first shot was in his chest, the second in his left arm. My third shot was behind his back.' Murray miraculously survived the attack. The gangster was sentenced on the 8 February in 1983 to six years; he is still there and will be for the rest of his life.

Given the strict secrecy code enforced by beatings and murder I was surprised the Number guys I'd met had told me as much as they had, but I wondered how I was going to find out any more. There was obviously a big macho thing in the Number – a man had to prove his courage, suffer in silence, all that – but from what I had gleaned so far, I suspected there was something much more intriguing they were keeping to themselves. Back in my nice hotel, after a hot curry and with a much-needed cold beer in my fist, I sat down to read more of what our researcher John Conway had found out.

I got a bit of a shock. The Number have a history, and what a history. One of the strangest, most violent and most sexualized gangs on earth, South Africa's Number gangsters trace their roots back through the apartheid system to the Zulu and Boer Wars.

Founded in 1906 by a bandit of Zulu origin named Nongoloza Mathebula, the Number gang started up in and around the settlements, mines and prisons of Johannesburg. Blessed with an extremely fertile imagination, Nongoloza invented a gang universe based around the three numbers that were magically important for him – 26, 27 and 28. Originally naming his followers the Ninevites after a biblical warrior tribe,

Nongoloza organized his gang along the military lines he had seen work so effectively for the British and the Boers. Nongoloza's soldiers might not have had real uniforms, but in their minds they had splendid ones based on British examples. For a time the Ninevites had stood up to God's will; in the same way the Number would stand up to the British and Boer invaders.

Along with imaginary uniforms came a paramilitary structure. Ranks and rules, hierarchies and codes of behaviour – magpie-like, Nongoloza picked from the military techniques he'd been exposed to in the recent wars. He and his men went underground, living in a series of disused mineshafts, caves and tunnels to the south-west of Johannesburg. Perhaps the punishing hit-and-run guerrilla tactics of the heavily outnumbered Boers, who had come inch-close to defeating the British army, inspired him. The gang's robberies, often from unarmed and defenceless mine workers, became a byword for brutality. The Ninevites, or Number as they gradually became known, terrorized the area surrounding their warrens for the best part of twenty years. All kinds of legends and myths grew up around Nongoloza and his gang: they had beautiful white women living in their subterranean fortresses; they had shops and ammunition magazines and armouries, food stores and workshops of every description. Nongoloza's followers believed he was bullet proof and had magical powers.

From the outset, there were three Number divisions:

the 28s were the gang's warriors, divided into the blood line, which did the fighting, and the white or private line, which was looked on as female. Imprisoned 28s were permitted to have ritualized sex with the white line. Kept in the dark and used at will, white line members were not told the whole of the gang's history and inner secrets.

I was learning, but I could see that only the Number themselves understood all of the gang's secrets, and perhaps even then only its most senior members. In Pollsmoor a 28 officer known as the *glas* (binoculars) is in charge of recruitment. The *glas* goes into the new arrivals area and selects likely-looking candidates for each of the Number divisions, as well as for specific roles within the gangs. Once he has chosen a prospect, the *glas* will ask the man a trick question: 'If you can have soft soap to wash with or rough soap, which will you choose?' If the man chooses soft, he will be made into a *wyfie*. The correct answer for a real man, of course, is rough. Another, more subtle example is 'If it is raining and you have an umbrella, would you share it with me?' The correct answer is 'No, I would come out in the rain with you.' They are looking for the smart cookies – recruits they believe have the right Number spirit. Also, if you share your umbrella, what else will you share.

Often originally sentenced to short terms of imprisonment, once made assassins there is no way out for the 27s: the more men he kills, the longer a 27 serves.

One man I spoke to had been sentenced to six years in February 1983. A quarter of a century later he was still accumulating more and more time. Any money the 26 earn by their trickery is shared between all three Number divisions. The only way of leaving the Number is to reverse the process by which you joined. If you came in with blood then you must leave with blood – kill your way out. If you are a 26 and you came in with money then you must give the Number the same amount of cash to quit. It is possible to leave the Number and move on to live outside the gang, but then it is also possible to win the national lottery.

Captured and imprisoned in 1912, Nongoloza told a prison warder, 'I reorganized my gang of robbers. I laid them under what has since become known as Nineveh law. I read in the Bible about the great state Nineveh which rebelled against the Lord and I selected that name for my gang as rebels against the government's laws.' Was Nongoloza a freedom fighter or a vicious armed robber? You decide.

Not all prisoners in Pollsmoor serve the Number gang as *wyfies*, only those unlucky enough to end up in a Number-dominated wing, but as in all prisons other types of sexual contact take place. Male transvestites, I discovered, can earn more money as prostitutes in Pollsmoor than outside. In my travels round the prison, I met some.

The first thing Beyoncé, Sandy and Charmaine told me was that the other prisoners looked on them as the only real women in Pollsmoor. As such, the 'girls' are given a lot of respect, and get a lot of work. Free to move around the prison without fear of harm, they also told me that some of the Number gangsters made use of their services, even though they already had their pick of *wyfies*.

When we met, Beyoncé, Sandy and Charmaine had just finished some business in the one-person cell they shared. This was unbelievably small, only as wide as my outstretched arms and no more than half a metre longer than that. Somehow, the prison authorities had managed to squeeze in a three-tier bunk. Beyoncé had a coarse ginger wig held in place with a black Alice band, Charmaine had tight, square-shaped plaits that looked suspiciously like hair extensions and Sandy wore a full-bottomed, blue-black wig that fell to her ample shoulders. In hot pants or tight jeans and high-heeled sandals, all three were festooned with flashy jewellery: rings, brightly coloured bangles, elaborate necklaces and dangly earrings. In complete contrast, they were also heavily tattooed. Given the lack of space, they explained that while one of them was entertaining a customer, the other two stood outside and chatted to waiting clients. The man who had bought some professional services just before we got there came out looking rather sheepish, but at the same time he had a big smile on his face.

The cell we squeezed into was decked out with garish wallpaper, scarves draped here and there and glossy magazine photographs pinned to the walls in what to me looked like a poignant attempt at home-making. There was an overpowering aroma of what I can only describe as man smells and cheap scent.

My first meeting with them was surreal but, I have to admit, dead funny. 'Hello,' said a burly figure with a pierced nose and a heavy Afrikaans lisp. 'My name's Beyoncé.' To prove it, she touched the big B tattooed on one side of her neck. Beyoncé had a lot of facial scarring from being beaten up by ungrateful clients, rivals, pimps and robbers. A large publicity shot of pop star Beyoncé Knowles, known both for her beauty and her ability to shake it, was tacked to the cell wall. Pointing to it with a flounce, Pollsmoor Beyoncé lisped, 'That is a picture of me before my plane crash. Look at my face now; it's a mess, isn't it? But people still fancy me.' She delivered this line with so much aplomb that we all laughed. Craig Matthew, our cameraman, laughed so much his glasses slipped off his forehead and dropped into the cell's open toilet pan. We all gathered round and looked down. Craig's specs were resting on top of something highly unpleasant. There was a short silence, followed by a long discussion about who was going to fish out the specs. We were all thinking the same thing.

'Who's going to get my glasses out?' Craig asked.

'Don't look at me,' I said hurriedly.

'Or me,' said Jeff Hodd, our soundman.

'We're not putting our hands down there,' the 'girls' lisped in chorus. Grim-faced, Craig set about retrieving his spectacles with a couple of pencils. Every time he succeeded in lifting them clear of the mess in the bowl, the glasses slipped back. After several more attempts Craig stood up, let out a long stream of curses and gave up, leaving the specs as a memento of our visit.

Saturday night in Pollsmoor is a cross between a rave, a Roman orgy and a barely contained riot. The prisoners watch rugby or some other sport in the afternoon, then, as evening comes on, start smoking crystal methamphetamine, or *tik* as they call it. As darkness falls and the chemicals start to hit, the noise levels go through the roof. I discovered this by standing in one of the prison exercise yards. It was like being close to an ugly football crowd, the ferocious din only slightly muted by the dead stone of the walls and the metal sheeting on the windows. I could understand why the neighbours might get upset. Fully drugged up by about 10 p.m., the gangsters switch the TVs to a soft porn channel. When this happens, the sex gets going. Afterwards, to come back down they smoke *dagga* – strong marijuana often laced with Mandrax or 'buttons' as it is locally known.

How is it the authorities tolerate this? While the ratio of prisoners to warders remains as it is, there isn't much else they can do. The soft porn, the drugs and the other 'privileges' act as a kind of collective tranquillizer. If the Number did not have their Saturday night specials to look forward to, there is every chance they would riot. And if three or four thousand of them did that, on past form a lot of people would get killed.

'The Number don't just control the other prisoners in Pollsmoor,' Malgas explained, 'they have access to illicit drugs, the best healthcare the South African prison system can provide, three square meals a day and a television.' Not only that, the gangsters enjoy a respect and status inside Pollsmoor prison far greater than they could ever hope to come by in the outside world, where they are just random faces in the criminal crowd. 'If they are not doing too well out on the streets,' Malgas added, 'some Number gangsters will go out and commit a serious crime to get back into Pollsmoor or another Number prison.' Having learned about the Number's Saturday night entertainment and the way they exercise total control over their slaves, bizarrely, the Number gang life on the inside is better than life outside.

Although the vast majority are guilty of crimes that include murder, robbery and rape, almost all Pollsmoor's prisoners go to church on Sunday morning. This is less in the hope of getting time off their sentences, and more for something to do while the 26s clean the blocks with disinfectant, bleach, mops, buckets and strong detergent after the riotous debauches of the previous night. Why the 26s? In the inscrutable inner workings of the Number gang, cleaning is one of their allotted tasks.

By that Sunday, on our fourth visit, inmates and staff had realized we were trying to paint an honest if warts-and-all picture of life inside. Perhaps because of this, I was granted an audience with one of the highest-ranking 28 'generals' in Pollsmoor. His name was John Mongrel. Mongrel's face and body had the look of oak. He wasn't the biggest gangster I had ever met, but a glance at his face told me he was the most evil. Mongrel looked as if he'd kill you without a second thought. Sentenced to nine years aged fourteen for murder, the general had spent nineteen years in Pollsmoor working his way to the top. The extra ten years he has so far served were for killing an inmate, the price of admission to the gang.

Looking into his eyes made me feel as if no human being should be allowed to see and do what Mongrel has seen and done. I felt I was in the company of a walking corpse, a man who had done so many bad things to so many people he had lost all connection with any human feelings he might ever have had.

Leaning forward, Mongrel clouded me in breath that could strip paint, a mixture of old ashtray, roadkill and ancient bodily fluids. It was like being in a block of poisoned air, making everything he came near wither and die. I was meeting Hannibal Lecter, only for real. And just like the fictional serial killer, Mongrel was scarily intelligent – the penetrating stare seemed to worm every last little thought from my brain.

He told me about his initiation into the gang. 'I went to the 28s. I was given a number. The other guy came, and I strangled him. Then I took the knife and stabbed him in his heart – two times until the blood came out.' Since that first murder, Mongrel told me, he was the one who gave the orders inside Pollsmoor. Including orders to kill. 'If there is a warder in the prison who is not right I tell the 27, "You are the 27 – here is a knife for you. You must kill the warder, or the major or the captain." And the 27 tells me, "Salute, my brother. I am going. You can watch." And then I go to the cell there, and I watch.'

'What would happen,' I asked, 'if a 27 didn't follow your orders?'

The bright unyielding gaze hardened. 'When they cannot stand for their duty, I kill them. We cannot stand for that.' Mongrel's rank gave him the confidence to speak openly about the Number where less senior members were too scared. I realized that this man had done far more than I would ever want to know.

Maintaining the thousand-metre stare you get from killing lots of people, Mongrel said he was the spider at the heart of the Pollsmoor web. When he pulled a string, the Number soldiers jumped to obey his instructions – beating, stabbing, raping and killing. As for him, he took anything and anyone he wanted. 'If a person comes in the cell and he is not the Number, my duty is to ask him what he is here for and how long. I tell him, "You sleep there." And if he is not the Number, I have sex with him.'

'How do you have sex with him? Do you hold him down?'

'I hold him down. My face to [his] face.'

'Does someone else help you hold him down or do you do it on your own?'

Mongrel shook his head. 'No, he's scared for me.'

I asked Mongrel whether the fact he had been having sex with men for nineteen years meant he was gay.

He glared at me. 'Not gay. I am *ndota* – a man.' *Ndota* is Zulu for warrior man.

'You're the man, but what about the man that gets fucked? What's he?'

The expression of contempt he wore deepened. 'He is a woman – a *wyfie*. A woman. I tell him, "You must wash my clothes." He do it, I give him bread, food. I give him a bed and watch him [to make sure] he's all right.'

'Do you have a ladyboy in here now?'

'I have one.'

'How long have you been with that one?'

'Three weeks.'

'Three weeks. Do you change them regularly?'

'Yes, I change.'

'You just walk up to them and you go, "You will be my wife"?'

'Yes. She comes sleep by me. By [in] my bed.'

'If they don't do that, what happens?'

'I kill them.'

Speaking with the kind of focus that can stop a truck, Mongrel told me how he turns an ordinary plastic toothbrush into a lethal weapon. 'You heat the end of the handle with a lighter until it is long and pointed and then you leave it to harden. When it is set in shape, you take the pointed end and you sharpen it by rubbing it against a stone floor until it turns into a dagger blade. Then you go to kill with it.'

The next bit is gruesome. While three other 28s hold him down, Mongrel sits astride his victim's chest. Then, he pushes the point of the sharpened toothbrush in between the ribs just above the man's heart, using both hands and all of his weight until it is wedged firmly in place. Then he stands, raises a foot and stamps down as hard as he can on the improvised dagger's handle. The point is rammed into the heart until, as Mongrel put it with a smack of the lips, 'the black blood comes out'.

Mongrel told me what happened after he stabbed his first warder to death. Placing him in the 'one-ones', solitary confinement, they came for him in the night and set about him with shovels, beating him repeatedly over the head until he was unconscious. He made me put my fingers on the top of his square skull. The plates of bone beneath the skin moved in a spongy way that was both weird and unnerving. I snatched my hand away. After the beating, Mongrel said, the guards had put him on a starvation diet of millet and water for over six weeks. Granny's birdseed to you and me, the human body cannot digest millet. You have to chew it over and over, pass it out in your stool, wash it with water if there's any to hand and then eat the stuff all over again. The second time round, the grain gives you just enough nourishment to stay alive. Except that by then you may not want to.

The scariest thing for me was his matter-of-factness, even when he was describing the most cold-blooded drawn-out murder. It's rare you meet someone you know is capable of doing anything, however bad, to his fellow human beings. John Mongrel was one of them.

One of the strangest things about being in South Africa was going back to my hotel after a day inside Pollsmoor. I kept noticing that in this country you are either fenced in or fenced out. Even my nice hotel – especially my nice hotel – was covered in a latticework of steel up to and including the window of my room on the first floor. The guests sitting next to me at breakfast didn't just lead a different life to the inmates of Pollsmoor; they were living on a different planet. Entering Pollsmoor was like leaving the world I knew and going down into some evil pit. Coming back out to the light again was just as unreal. Mongrel wanted me to know in detail how he dominated his victims; the hotel guests wanted me to admire their big flashy cars or their big flashy mistresses or whatever else they owned that made them feel important. Many were mid-thirties Brits who had made their pile in the City of London and then retired to the sun and the promise of a perfect life to find themselves living in a gated community – with fences round it higher than those surrounding Pollsmoor and armed response on call 24/7.

The Number is a prison gang but to understand it I needed to visit the place where almost all of its members had been born and grown up, the Cape Flats. With only a few ways in and out, the entire twenty-five by eighteen-kilometre area can be locked down by the police and the army at will. Much like Pollsmoor. A badly policed warren of ugly housing blocks, rock-bottom housing projects, shanties, shacks and cardboard tents, the Cape Flats is home to about two million of South Africa's poorest people. Despite some government attempts to improve things, one in three of the shanties is still without sanitation, power or running water. Parts of it reminded me of Rio de Janeiro's favelas. My guide for this part of the programme was Kevin, a junior boss in the 5,000-strong Americans gang.

Driving through this huge area, I didn't need Kevin to tell me that the shanty towns and shacks of the Cape Flats are seriously infested with gangs. Everyone in South Africa knows about the Flats, and their fame – or notoriety – has spread around the world. There are some 200 gangs operating there currently, their territories often separated by nothing more than a single street. Like the gangs I saw in St Louis and Brazil, they spend a lot of their time fighting one another for control of turf. The biggest and best organized drugs gangs in the Flats are the Americans and the Firm, but larger gangs also include the Sexy Boys, the Junkey Funkeys, the West Siders, the Ghetto Boys, the Hard Livings and the Dixies.

What do the Flats gangs have to do with the Number? When harder drugs like crystal methamphetamine began appearing on the market in the 1980s, the closed, inward-looking world of the Number began to change. Easier to sell than marijuana and yielding a much bigger profit, hard drugs brought with them a whole new raft of Flats gangsters made rich by the trade. With much wider horizons and much bigger ideas, some of these outside gangsters started ending up in jail. Big men on their own turf, inside prisons like Pollsmoor the high flyers, as they call gang bosses here on the Cape, got a big shock. They had no power. Even worse, the Number viewed them as potential slaves. Rather than serve out their prison time as *wyfies*, the high flyers paid out huge sums of money to join the Number. As soon as that happened, the Cape Flats gangsters began to corrupt and undermine the Number code. To take just two examples, the Number excused them from brutal initiation beatings and did not require the high flyers to kill or injure a warder before joining. In return, the high flyers gave some of the Number generals access to and jobs in the drugs trade.

Before the Cape Flats drug bosses started to join, the Number never ever operated outside the sealed world of South Africa's prisons, but when the high flyers and their followers left prison, they took bits of the Number code they had learned on the inside out onto the streets. Changing the name of its leaders from high flyers to generals, members of the Cape Flats gang that calls itself the Firm, for example, have aligned themselves with the blood line of the 28s. For their part, the Americans, like Kevin, have adopted the rituals and beliefs of the 26s.

Copying the high flyers and fancying themselves hard men of the Number, young Cape Flats gangsters took up and ran with its ideology. They were now *ndota*s, male Zulu warriors imitating the feared and respected Number prison gangsters. To these aspiring young bloods, everyone outside the gang on the Flats, every taxi and bus driver, every shopkeeper or citizen, was a *frans*: a subhuman to be beaten, murdered, raped and robbed. As the days and weeks go by, the gangs are extending their influence and reach across the Cape.

A sad-faced loose-limbed thirty-two-year-old American gang member who was also a sergeant in the 26s, Kevin's right eyelid was partially stuck open as a result of a wound he had come by from a burning tyre when he was young. He had served several years in Pollsmoor for various offences and took me to meet about a dozen of his fellow American gang members at a place they had nicknamed, with heavy irony, the White House.

This was a low-ceilinged claustrophobic shed that had once been whitewashed. It was decked out with bits and pieces of US paraphernalia: photographs torn from the pages of magazines, posters and a small tattered Stars and Stripes. Inside were seven or eight men who had clearly been drinking and taking drugs before we arrived. The moment I appeared, they started on the *tik*.

To smoke the *tik*, Kevin and his mates took a light bulb, heated it up and blew the glass until the bulb end ballooned out into a shape they called a lollipop. Burning a small hole in the top of this, the Americans carefully sucked a small amount of *tik* up from its bag with a straw, dropped the meth crystals into the lollipop, heated the bulb with a lighter and smoked the fumes. As if that wasn't enough for a night out with the lads, between hits of *tik* the gang smoked strong marijuana laced with Mandrax – 'buttons'. Taking the neck of a broken bottle, they scraped its edges until they were smooth, packed the neck with marijuana, crushed Mandrax buttons over the top, mixed it into the dope with a thin stick, set the whole lot alight and pulled hard. The idea was to rollercoast between a huge amphetamine high and a massive downer. It was as if they were hurtling in a high-speed lift to the fifteenth floor, swapping elevators and then plunging back down to sub-level thirteen.

Consequently, these were not healthy human beings. Drug abuse had softened their facial bones, giving many of them a kind of budgerigar look. Still no more than twenty or thirty years old, most also had big boils on their faces and gums. In this close little room full of gangsters and powerful chemicals, I was keen to keep a clear head and ask at least a couple of intelligent questions but in seconds I started to feel the dizzying effects of the fumes.

As the *tik* took hold, the Americans started talking. Many of the photographs on the walls were of black US gangsta rappers but that didn't mean they liked black South Africans. One man, the most articulate of the group, said, 'I'm not ashamed to be a Cape Coloured, but it seems to me we're third now. You can count how many coloured people you find in parliament. The African people are the majority in parliament. When we went to school, every one of us had a dream. We wanted to become something in life. Now we're getting lower and lower.' Judging by the murmurs of agreement, that was the general perception. In fact, under recent so-called upliftment laws all South African employers must have workforces that are 50 per cent black, 30 per cent 'coloured' and 20 per cent white.

By the time I finally got out of the White House I felt sick and zoned out from secondary inhalation. God knows what it is like taking a full hit of crystal meth and then dousing it with buttons and dope. No wonder these guys were unstable and prone to acts of random violence. After drinking about four or five pints of water, I fell into bed at seven in the evening. It was eight o'clock the next day before I came round.

As we got to know each other, Kevin introduced me to his sister Janice. Doing her best to raise her son and keep him out of the gangs despite having a gang leader brother, Janice was definitely one of the good guys. And that is something the outside world needs to know about the Cape Flats. Thousands of people there are trying to lead honest, productive lives. There are all kinds of self-help and community groups trying to improve things. It's just that, with so many gangsters at work all around, living honestly is hard. After we'd been chatting in her mother's clean, well-organized kitchen for a while, Janice told me why Kevin always looked so sad. 'Thirteen years ago, Kevin came home one evening with a cocked gun – illegal of course. His six-month-old son found it in the morning. The gun went off and he died on the way to hospital.'

When she learned of her child's death, Kevin's devastated wife left him and started dating a fellow gangster. During a hit allegedly intended for the new boyfriend, she too was shot dead. The people responsible have never been caught.

I asked Kevin about his son's death. At first he told me the gun had 'been in the wrong place' and tried to justify his stupidity: 'Some guns don't have safeties.' But eventually his hard-man shell cracked and he began to cry. His son had been the light of his life, he told me with tears streaming down his face. 'He was in my arms when he died.' He told me how much he wanted to be reunited with his wife and son, and how he still believed in God. 'I'll be living in peace when I die because I'm ready to straighten my path for the next life. If God makes a promise he won't break it. Even if I don't meet them, I will be there with him. The best is your family and your relatives.' With a mum who runs the local softball team and a sister who is one of the nicest people I have ever met, on the face of it my new acquaintance had had every chance to grow up straight. Until, that is, you discover that his father had been a general in the 26s.

In a bedroom of the small breeze-block house he shared with his mother, Kevin showed me his arsenal of weapons. Kevin and an American gangster friend who was also there kept their firearms scrupulously clean, not just to maintain them in working order but to remove any fingerprints. The friend didn't want to be named but was willing to show me the terrible injuries to his stomach, backside and a leg that he had suffered when a rival gangster shot him at close range with hollow-point bullets. His leg looked like the branch of a tree that has been split down the middle with an axe and then miraculously grown back together; a lot of his backside was shot away and he had been obliged to excrete into a colostomy bag for more than a year through a second, bullet-created navel.

Kevin and the rest of the gang coat their hands with wood glue before going out on the streets with their guns. The glue forms a kind of second skin which the gangsters believe stops them leaving fingerprints or

DNA traces. Speaking of weapons, Kevin suddenly reached down under the bed, pulled out a beautiful antique Martini-Henry rifle that dated back to the Boer War and urged me to buy it. I declined the offer. He told me that even when the police caught him with a firearm, all he had to do was pay them a bribe of 100–150 rand (about ten pounds) and they would let him go.

Before going back to the city, I met Paul Manuel, a South African Police Service (SAPS) inspector trying to steer some of the local boys away from a life of crime by setting up and running a boxing club. Having as a police officer dealt directly with Kevin, Manuel left me in no doubt that he was one of the worst gangsters at large on the Cape Flats. He implied that under the old regime people like Kevin would have been dealt with in a much more direct way. When I asked Manuel what was so bad about Kevin in particular, he told me a very upsetting story. 'All over the Cape Flats are these taverns – drinking dens, very dangerous places to be around – filled with drunk drugged-up armed gangsters looking for their next opportunity.' Manuel said a lot of the gangsters who haunt these places deliberately set out to get young local girls hooked on *tik*. Once hooked, these '*tik* ghosts' slip out of the house when their parents are asleep and go looking for the drug. Gangsters like Kevin are willing to supply the crystal meth in return for sex – and gang-rape the girls if they don't get it.

*

Leaving South Africa, I felt a mix of sadness and hope. From what I had known about the Number gang before actually meeting any of them, I hadn't been expecting a country picnic, but the reality was much worse than I could have imagined. South Africa is a beautiful country with so much going for it. Many of the most disadvantaged people are trying to turn things to the good. But after thirteen years of ANC rule, crime is as bad as it ever was and gang violence both inside and outside the country's prisons is rife. The gap between rich and poor is still vast; one elite has simply taken over from another. But while people like Chris Malgas and Paul Manuel exist, the Rainbow Nation may yet find its crock of gold.

6. Moscow

Made a showcase city under Tsarist and communist rule, Moscow is big, bright and beautiful to look at. Both Lenin and Stalin understood the value of building on the grand scale. The state architecture is massive and imposing, while the boulevards are broad enough to take a victorious army. Even the Metro – especially the Metro – is magnificent, putting London's grimy, inefficient and expensive Underground to shame. With one of the fastest-growing economies in the world and a new business elite grown rich since the fall of the Soviet regime, the city's clubs, bars and watering holes make it one of the world's best party towns. This is a city of broad views and handsome prospects, but it is also home to some very unpleasant gangs. Despite the many attractions on offer, I was there to find out about one of them.

The main reasons for looking at the Moscow neo-Nazis was that I wanted to investigate a gang based purely on ideology, in this case an extreme racist Nazi ideology. The first place I looked was on the Internet. In seconds the search engine came back with a long list of extreme right-wing Russian websites, many of them including the number 18. The first letter of the alphabet is A and the eighth, H. You guessed it – Adolf Hitler. To many people with extreme right-wing views these otherwise innocent letters hold almost mystical significance. A lot of gangs and websites also use 88, the numbers for the initial letters of the Nazi salute 'Heil Hitler'.

Lots of websites showed skinhead thugs who had obviously been trained to attack people they didn't like. One gang stood out from the rest in my trawl. It called itself the National Socialist Union (NSO). In Moscow our translator Elena called the contact telephone number. A male voice on the other end said the gang would be happy to let us film them. Having spent a couple of days wandering about chatting to people, I had already begun to suspect that like Moscow's sex workers, its racist gangs operated more openly than they do in the UK.

The National Socialist Union invited us to meet them at a downtown Moscow gym run by gang leader Dimitri Rumyansev. A shabby, ill-equipped upstairs room in a monolithic former Soviet-era office block, the gym provides free training in 'street fighting' to anyone who signs up to its neo-Nazi world view. There was something not quite finished about Rumyansev: the pebbly grey eyes looked as if they had been pressed into the pasty face as an afterthought. At the same time his expression suggested that here was a man who would not just follow orders, he would give them too.

Placing one hand on his hip in classic Nazi functionary

style, he threw me a Nazi salute, as if he fancied himself the new Heinrich Himmler. In his early forties, Rumyansev, who seemed to have had a charisma bypass operation, claimed nevertheless to be in charge of the gang's ideology and propaganda. No sooner had we started talking than he hinted of dark deeds to come: 'We train the people who are going to take part in momentous events in the future. We train our people for combat.' Skinheads, he told me, are especially welcome.

Where good leaders inspire by example and lead from the front, Rumyansev stood back and watched the training. Much more media savvy than most gangsters I had met, Rumyansev made it clear that as far as he was concerned any publicity was good publicity, as long as he controlled exactly what his followers said on camera. Tongue wedged firmly in cheek I asked him, 'What would you do if any Muslims applied to join the gang?'

After thinking this over for a few seconds he said seriously, 'This has not happened yet.' So it wasn't just the charisma that was missing. Rumyansev summed up the gang's ideology: 'We understand that street violence alone does not solve the problem of the immigrants. Direct violence must go hand in hand with a political revolution. Then we can stop any more of these people coming in, and get rid of the ones who are already in Russia. When a person understands that, he leaves the skinheads and comes to us.' Even leaving aside the fact he had not specified exactly what he meant by 'get rid of', I found Rumyansev's frankness alarming.

The actual combat training we could see taking place came down to a series of short sharp lessons in how to beat up innocent citizens. At the time of our visit it was being supervised by Sergei Malyuta, a stocky hard-packed ex-paratrooper who had never heard the words soap or deodorant. This was a pity, as he fancied himself as something of a ladies' man. All I can say is, if I were a lady – or for that matter a wildebeest – I'd want to stay at least half a mile upwind.

The people in the gym consisted for the most part of former Russian army soldiers providing the training, almost all of whom had fought in Chechnya, and Muscovites in their teens and early twenties. The trainee group was mostly made up of guys who would not have been picked by either side in a playground football match. What surprised me was the mix of social classes punching and kicking the bags. The stereotype neo-Nazi is a poor, white, disaffected working-class youth, but here was Sasha, a good-looking twenty-year-old economics student from a wealthy Moscow family, doing her best to give the punchbags a pounding. Sasha looked as if her own ethnic origins might lie in one of the 'stans' – Kazakhstan, Turkmenistan, Tajikistan or Uzbekistan. Slim and fit in a khaki cropped top and shorts that immediately made our cameraman Andy Thomson dub her Lara Croft, Sasha was also articulate, charming and rather pretty. Maybe that had helped her circumvent NSO rules, but it was a bit of a mystery why she would want to.

Sitting her down among the graffiti, mess and mud for an interview on a comfy improvised bench of collapsed concrete pillars outside, it became clear that Sasha had not just been drawn in by the chance of hunky men, some excitement and learning a few unarmed combat moves. Introduced to the gang by her elder brother, she truly believed in the NSO cause. 'The situation in Russia is unstable,' she told me with a shy and slightly nervy smile. 'This is why survival skills will be very important . . . I think a civil war may break out between the people who realize the country is in a critical situation' – she waved a slender arm to indicate her fellow neo-Nazis – 'and the people who don't care.' Her notion of the enemy seemed vague, to say the least, but she had definitely swallowed the party line.

The ex-soldiers told me how they had all lost friends fighting the Chechens. They had learned their hatred of anyone who was not 'pure white Russian' – especially Muslims – in the process. One of the scary things about the gang was that while a few of its members were from deprived backgrounds, most held down reasonably well-paid day jobs and trained to be neo-Nazis in their spare time. It was kind of like Dad's Army for fascists, only with teenage recruits and a whole lot more serious.

Most of Moscow's immigrants come from one of the former Soviet republics. The right-wing gangs call them blacks, or, not to be coy about it, the Russian equivalent of niggers. During the days when their countries formed part of the Soviet Union, these mainly economic refugees had seen the occupying Russians as a separate, much richer and more socially successful class. Even Red Army soldiers had roubles to splash around. Not surprisingly, once the internal travel restrictions that existed under communism were lifted, many of the poor people in these former colonies set off in search of a better life – and where better to try than the capital of the empire that had ruled them for so long? After all, they had been forced to learn Russian in school, pay lip-service to communist ideology, watch Russian television and take regular doses of Russian culture. The incomers you see walking Moscow's streets are mostly Tajiks, Kazakhs and Armenians fleeing ethnic or political persecution in their home countries or trying to achieve a better standard of living.

To see if I was hard enough and deserved greater access to its inner mysteries, the NSO took me to a never-completed hospital on the grim northern outskirts of the city. As we pitched up outside to begin my 'urban training', the first thing I noticed was a gang of Tajiks resurfacing the road opposite. This struck me as something of an irony: many of the right-wing gangs make it clear on their websites how happy they are to attack and even kill immigrants, but then who is going to do all the hard low-paid work? At this moment Sasha arrived in a brand new Volkswagen Beetle which must have cost five times the combined annual wages of the road menders and needed their skills to save its suspension from the local crop of potholes. I was in danger of irony overload.

A six-storey, crumbling concrete shell that had originally been white but was now slowly turning mud grey, the hospital had been commissioned, half built and then left to rot. This happens a lot in today's shiny new capitalist Moscow. The object of the exercise is to channel money to the contractors, especially the concrete suppliers. Of course, everyone in the loop, as often as not including local government officials, gets a nice fat bung. These ghost projects are also sometimes used to launder criminally acquired money.

The whole building leaked like the rose of a watering can. Here and there the gangs who used it for training had sprayed 'white power' Celtic cross symbols on the walls. Months later I would realize that they were just like those used by similar neo-Nazi gangs on the other side of the world, in Orange County, California. Melted snow had run down the supporting pillars and walls and collected in the basement, turning most of it into a freezing, stagnant lake. The concrete had been poor quality in the first place; now it was eroding like a lump of ageing Swiss cheese the whole place was a death trap. The gaping holes in the floors were big enough even for me to fall through. Thick wire reinforcing rods stuck up all over the place, and parts of the outside walls were missing, leaving long, sheer drops to the ground below. As I fought my way through the head-high Japanese knotweed that was rapidly turning the area into a wilderness, I realized that the NSO guys with me took this deadly seriously. For a start they were all wearing camouflage gear. I'd never really imagined myself running around a building site with a bunch of neo-Nazis, but suddenly it felt as if it mattered.

The first exercise, Rumyansev explained, was 'fitness training', in the form of a five-kilometre assault course. This entailed several circuits of a route that wound up, down, inside and around the hospital. But Rumyansev was not going to do the course personally – maybe he had a letter from his mum. Sizing the place up, I realized the lack of any interior electric lighting meant we would be plunging from bright daylight into pitch darkness and back out again – that ought to make running round a total ruin more interesting.

Sergei Malyuta had warned me this would be the hardest day of my life, but I don't mind a bit of exercise now and again, and in a funny way I was quite looking forward to the challenge. I stripped off and climbed into a set of army trousers, laced my boots tight and politely declined the backpack containing ten bricks that the younger male gang members, in good macho style, now strapped across their shoulders. These boys were half my age. I didn't feel the need to prove myself and it looked like it was going to be hard enough.

We ran through scrub, rubble and brambles around the hospital's perimeter for what felt like hours in the blazing July heat before turning into the gloomy shell.

Having looked on the whole thing so far as merely painful, I changed my mind when we had to jump into the chest-deep freezing water in the dank basement. After the sweaty heat outside, the shock was enough to stop the heart. But there was no time to die; we had to wade on, doing our best not to come a cropper on the invisible wire rods beneath the black water, climb out the other side and keep up with our appointed leader, Artiem, a rat-faced, wiry youth who fancied himself as a hard guy. I disliked the man on sight, and he made it obvious the feeling was mutual.

My swift recce of the hospital's interior now proved accurate: the sudden alternation of darkness and dazzling sunlight gave the eyes almost no time to adjust to hazards. We were running hard across the fourth floor, dodging in and out of the crumbling pillars, me just about keeping up with the Nazi youth directly ahead and in an odd way not completely hating it. Spotting pools of water gleaming in the gloom up ahead I thought, That's fine, I can see that. Either splash through or go round, but keep going. Don't fall behind.

Wooden pallets covered some of the bigger and more dangerous holes. Good job, I thought, puffing along at full tilt. Looking down, I noticed my boots had picked up a thick caking of mud. Maybe this was slowing me down. Given my heart rate, it was worth finding out. A pallet in front of me had been laid over what looked like a large puddle. I was starting to feel more than a little knackered – definitely a good idea to scrape off the mud. I stopped dead. Placing my right boot on the edge of the pallet, I put my weight on it and drew the sole back to scrape it clean.

The pallet did not span a puddle of water; it was covering a huge hole in the rotten concrete. As I leaned forward, the whole thing gave way under my weight and the wooden platform, with me on it, started falling through the floor. Feeling myself dropping into empty space the adrenalin kicked in. With a convulsive jerk I threw myself backwards. Landing on my backside about a metre away, I sat there for a few seconds staring at the yawning gap where the floor had just been and thinking two things: one, I was lucky to be alive; two, it would have been pretty dumb to die in an unfinished hospital. Still, to this day, I have no idea how I pulled off the back flip.

Our cameraman, Andy Thomson, who had, not surprisingly, been having trouble keeping up what with all the extra weight on his shoulder, lurched up next to me. He hadn't filmed it, but he'd seen my brush with unscheduled free fall. Andy looked down through the gap at the dark ground four storeys below strewn with pieces of smashed pallet. 'That's the closest you've come so far to killing yourself, Ross.' This got series producer Clive Tulloh thinking. The next gig was supposed to be abseiling down the hospital walls, but for me this was now vetoed on safety grounds.

Naturally the gang, especially Artiem, decided I was therefore a useless, spineless foreigner who had bottled it, so when we came to the third part of the day's training, billed as the 'duel', I was keen to prove him wrong. As Artiem explained, this was in preparation for the coming neo-Nazi revolution. 'Then,' he said earnestly, 'we will have to take arms and prove that we are men.' I asked who it was he thought the gang would be fighting. 'The most likely enemies are the army who Dimitri described as weak – and the Muslims,' he said, 'the people who come to occupy our land but want to impose their own beliefs on us. There are many enemies.' I tried not to laugh at the notion of Artiem leading any kind of revolution against the Russian state, but he caught me smiling and scowled his displeasure. Like most people who hold such views, the NSO gangsters were in deadly earnest.

The live firing exercise turned out to be a series of classic two-person duels, fought with powerful gas-powered pistols that shot small solid steel ball bearings. To make sure we understood how dangerous these were, Rumyansev and Artiem got me to fire at plastic bottles filled with water set up on the hospital roof. Sure enough, even from a distance of several metres the ball bearings went through the bottles of water and straight out the other side. They weren't going to kill you, but you sure as hell wouldn't want one to hit you in the eye. I handed the pistol back. I had fired air guns before as a kid, but these were in a different class.

Up we all trooped to the third floor, where the duelling was to take place. First up was Sasha, along with one of the younger guys. They squared up back to back. Dimitri counted to three; the duo walked five paces, turned and fired. Or at least the guy did – Sasha simply dodged about squealing. When Rumyansev asked her why she had failed to return fire, she admitted sheepishly she had forgotten to release the pistol's safety catch. Lucky the promised revolution wasn't quite upon us yet.

My own opponent was my very good enemy Artiem. He had a crafty little smirk on his face I did not much like the look of but, hey, I had a pistol too. Besides, in preparation for a previous television show I had done a fair bit of weapons training, courtesy of Chris Ryan and some other ex-SAS guys. I'm no James Bond, but I was reasonably confident of hitting Artiem at least once if I got the chance. I have to admit I was also quite looking forward to getting him some place where it hurt. I could tell the feeling was mutual.

We made ready, donning goggles, gloves and basic motocross-style balaclavas. But then the gang sprang a little surprise: to add a little extra zing to our duel we were first to be doused in petrol and set on fire. That had not happened to Sasha and her opponent. 'Give the man a gun!' someone shouted in guttural Russian. A gang member splashed petrol over my boots and down the back of my jacket then set fire to it. I felt the flames creep up my legs and curl over the small of my back. Things were warming up nicely.

We squared up back to back, just as men settling

scores would have done in the old days. While Rumyansev looked on like the Cheshire cat, Sergei Malyuta
counted down. 'Three, two, one, Go!'

On 'Go!' I turned, aimed and fired at the dodging
Artiem. I was pulling the trigger like a madman but
nothing happened. I had no ammunition. But, as I now
found to my cost, Artiem's pistol had a full mag. I
ducked and weaved as he fired, doing my best to avoid
the ball bearings winging past me and ricocheting off
the manky concrete walls.

Sadly, I'm no Keanu Reeves. My weapons training
never included the *Matrix* slo-mo bullet dodge. As I
swivelled neatly – at least I thought it was neat – a ball
bearing hit me smack in the chest. A second pinged me
in the ribs. I felt their impact all right, but neither shot
did me much damage. Then I felt a sharp, stinging pain
in my right forefinger. Now that did hurt.

Meanwhile, I was still on fire.

It seemed like a good time to put myself out. Luckily,
at this moment Artiem ran out of ammunition. I rolled
on the ground to douse the flames which by now were
singeing my ears – the Nazis helped to put the fire out,
I think they enjoyed stamping it out as much as setting
fire to me.

'Are you all right, Mr Kemp?' Rumyansev asked me
with the same crafty grin as his mate.

'Fine,' I replied through gritted teeth. 'Never better.
That was great fun, except that I didn't have any ammunition in my pistol.'

They treated me to a pantomime exchange of surprised looks, confirming my suspicion that I had been set up. My finger was throbbing where the ball bearing had smashed into it, but I was determined not to let them see how much it ached. When they went off to discuss the next exercise, I pulled my glove off to look at the damage. The round had whacked into the left side of my right index finger, raising a button of flesh that was already turning hard. From Russia with hate, I still have the lump.

All of this running about and play-fighting felt a bit like being in the Boy Scouts, but as the day wore on I realized that no matter how repellent the gang and its ideology, this kind of adventure training bonds people tight. It forges them into a unit and infuses them with team spirit, just as it did for the 'blond beast' cohorts of the Hitler Youth. Despite my best efforts to stand well back and keep a firm grip on my senses; after dodging the bricks that rained past my head from badly fastened backpacks; while wading through waist-deep freezing water; avoiding death by a whisker; getting set on fire; having my finger whacked and boosting my fellow trainees over walls, even I was beginning to feel a part of the group. A feeling I managed easily to quash the minute I met Edik and Irina Satenik.

Originally from Nagorno-Karabakh, a mainly Armenian enclave in Azerbaijan, the Sateniks were a pleasant, hard-working and intelligent couple who had fled their homeland after repeated attacks at the hands of militant Azerbaijanis, bent on ethnic cleansing. That was bad enough, but that wasn't what I had met them to talk about. With great courage, given the potential threat to their safety, the Sateniks told us their shocking story. Shortly before we arrived in Moscow a group of neo-Nazis had set upon their son Arta as he was travelling home from college on the train. While one member of the unidentified gang kept watch, two others jumped Arta without warning. They stabbed him six times in the neck with a knife. According to eyewitnesses, one of the pair shouted 'Glory to Mother Russia!' as he stabbed. There in the railway carriage eighteen-year-old Arta Satenik bled out his life.

'He was such a skinny boy,' a still distraught Irina Satenik told me. 'He had a very thin neck. What was there to cut up? But they stabbed him six times in the neck.'

With quiet dignity, Edik added, 'What for? Why my son, whom I raised, to whom I gave all my love, all my tenderness. Why did this non-human kill my son? A real man would never attack from behind. Only traitors, only weaklings do it. A strong person would never behave like that. The people who hide them are also weak. They teach people to attack secretly; they never say things to your face. They are rats. They are cowards.'

Since the attack Mrs Satenik will not allow her remaining son to travel anywhere by public transport, but to get to work she herself has to travel the same line her son was riding the day he died. Now, Irina Satenik wants to quit Russia, a country she hoped would be a safe haven from racist thugs. The Moscow police have carried out an investigation, but to date no one has been charged with Arta's murder.

The day after hearing Arta Satenik's story, I met a friend of Dimitri Rumyansev. Also calling himself Dimitri but unwilling to give his surname, this man described himself as an author. The book in question – 'book' dignifies a thing that does not deserve the description – was a graphic and very badly written account of a skinhead attack on a young immigrant woman. Innocent of any crime or offence, the defence-less young woman dies. The excerpt the proud Dimitri quoted to me out loud read, 'Why the fuck did you come here, bitch? Die, die, die!' Dimitri the writer was delighted with the effect his disgusting tirade was having on Russia's far-right thugs. 'Since the book was published,' he said, 'victims are not just beaten up; they are stabbed to death. People are using my book as an instruction manual.'

While most Muscovites are not racist, the idea that immigrants are taking their jobs is fairly widespread in the capital. One of the craziest things about neo-Nazi Russian gangs is that they seem to have forgotten that Hitler, the biggest Nazi of all time, killed some twenty million of their fellow countrymen in World War II, laid waste to huge areas of the Russian motherland and came very close to making Russia a German colony. All of this is somehow overlooked, and the German Nazis' key message – that everyone and anyone who did not exactly fit their notion of racial purity merited enslavement or extermination – has become the gospel of the neo-fascist Moscow gangs. Hitler held Slavs in the same contempt as he did everyone else who was not 'pure Aryan'. Maybe the gangsters don't know . . .

The alarming thing that distinguishes gangs like the NSO from others I looked at around the world is the fact that they enjoy at least verbal support from members of the establishment. The most outspoken of these supporters is Nikolai Kuryanovich, who agreed to meet up and talk. I turned up for the interview in my usual jeans and T-shirt, only to be told that Member of the State Parliament Kuryanovich was far too important and grand to talk to anyone not wearing a tie. So I had to go out and buy one. Once I had passed the clothing inspection, I then had to negotiate Kuryanovich's bodyguards, who checked our passports and permissions not once, not twice, but three times.

Just before the meeting I asked our researcher Marta Shaw, who had already met him, what Kuryanovich was like. Uncharacteristically, Marta hesitated. 'He's all right,' she said at last.

'All right? What does that mean? What does he look like?'

This produced another reflective silence. 'Well . . . he's quite nice-looking.' I studied Marta for a moment.

She was telling me something in code; I just hadn't understood it yet. When we were finally admitted into Member Kuryanovich's presence, the penny dropped. Stocky, round-faced and with a very close-shaven head, Kuryanovich looked a fair bit like me. Only no jeans.

The first thing I noticed in Kuryanovich's office was the large number of double-headed eagles dotted around, including a big brass example on his desk. A stuffed one perched on the wall above his head. As we went through the ritual of meeting and greeting, I found myself playing spot the eagle. I began to feel a little light-headed. There were eagles everywhere – it was an eagle convention. The stuffed eagle had landed. Enough eagles already. Yet more of these ancient symbols of Mother Russia – and ironically enough but with just one head – soared in majestic flight in the pictures and photographs plastered across the office walls. All of which made me think Kuryanovich might be a patriot. As if to scotch any lingering doubt about that, a large shot of a Hind-D helicopter gunship, the type Soviet forces used to kill thousands in the Russo-Afghan war, seemed to hint at a certain nationalist frame of mind.

To get the conversational ball rolling, Kuryanovich informed me that the leaders he most admired in history were Hitler and Stalin. Given they had been mortal enemies, this pairing struck me as strange. It was as if any old dictator would do, provided he was 'strong'. Strong enough to murder millions? Kuryanovich said he liked the books and films produced by the leaders of the Third Reich, projecting the 'unity of the nation', 'spirituality' and 'imperial power'.

Among many pieces of legislation Member Kuryanovich was trying to enact was one stipulating that any white Russian woman caught going out with a 'black' – as he termed immigrants – should be stripped of her passport. In Russia having no passport amounts to socio-economic death: no job, no freedom to travel, no civil rights, no nothing. The 'black' boyfriend, meanwhile, should be sent to the salt mines (no kidding) and made to work for the motherland. Kuryanovich called this 'mild slavery' without specifying the exact degree of mildness or otherwise. He also proposed the public execution by hanging of all corrupt Duma representatives. When I suggested he might rapidly run out of hooks, Kuryanovich gave me a crocodile grin: 'The supply of suitable equipment will not be a problem.'

It is hard to overstate how out of place the neo-Nazi gangsters' small and vicious ideology feels in a city as beautiful as Moscow. It is stunning to look at, and unless you happen to be an immigrant or penniless – or both – a great place to be. And there's the rub: in common with other countries plagued by a serious gang problem, modern Russia is a society sharply divided between the small number of haves and an extremely large number of have-nots. Wherever I went looking, the same basic truth stared me straight in the face: the greater the social divide, the worse the country's gang problem. In Moscow, also a city of grey monolithic housing blocks named after one or other of its grey, monolithic leaders, the poverty-stricken walk the same streets as billionaires. This was brought home to me at the upscale hotel where the crew and I stayed during the shoot.

One of the shops there did a nice line in Fabergé. Its precious metal and jewelled confections were made originally for the tsars and are now perhaps the ultimate symbol of wealth for Moscow's nouveau riche. I was browsing one day when a showily dressed middle-aged bottle blonde swept in with two younger sidekicks in tow. Perhaps they were her daughters – I didn't ask. Down to their scarlet lipstick and absurdly high heels, the younger women looked as if they had been cloned from the elder. As I watched from a postcard gondola, they bought the shop's entire stock of Fabergé goods, down to the last diamond-encrusted egg. When they had left, ushered to their waiting stretch limo by fawning attendants, I asked the shop's manager how much the trio had spent. Shrugging his shoulders as if this kind of thing happened every day, he replied, 'Oh, maybe a couple of million US dollars.'

In the new, free market Russia life revolves around corruption – bribery is the norm, and very little gets done without money changing hands. There is always something going on beneath the surface. One woman I met summed it up nicely. Were things really very different since the fall of the old regime? She cocked her head to one side and said, 'Under capitalism man exploits man. Under communism it is the other way round.' Moscow humour – dry as a bone. During the two weeks or so I spent in the city I grew to like Moscow and its people – with the exception of its right-wing gangsters – so much that, while I wouldn't want to spend the rest of my life there, I wouldn't mind spending a couple of years in the city living it up.

The next person I interviewed was a human rights lawyer from Tajikistan known as Gavahar. Gavahar has built a dangerous career out of specializing in immigrant race-hate crimes. She told us that while not all Moscow police officers are corrupt, many view foreigners as fair game.

All Metro stations and most other transport nodes have a dedicated police station. The police who man them routinely stop immigrants – or anyone they don't like the look of – to demand papers, passports and permits. If the person fails to produce the necessary documents, especially the crucial Moscow resident's permit, then one of two things happens: they are either arrested or they have to pay. The going bribe for immediate release is twenty US dollars. That's about a month's wages for a Moscow labourer and an unsustainable tax on a worker's daily commute. As a variant on this scam, once they have identified an illegal immigrant some police officers extort a weekly 'tax' from the victim's almost invariably pitiful wages.

If they resist the extortion, the police threaten to fit up illegal immigrants by planting drugs on them or trumping up some other charge. Gavahar said her office takes on an average of a hundred cases of racially motivated attacks and other anti-immigrant crimes every year, and struggles to get the Moscow authorities to take them seriously. 'Convictions,' she told me, 'are extremely rare.'

For obvious reasons it was hard to get victims to talk to me. One man brave enough to go on the record was 'Rostam'. Travelling home on the Metro one night, Rostam and his friend were stopped by a drunken police officer who demanded to see his papers. Rostam explained he had left them at home that day, but could get them and bring them back. The officer called for backup. Two other policemen took Rostam and his mate to the special little room the Moscow police have in every single Metro station. Once there, the officer who had stopped Rostam in the first place demanded twenty dollars. Rostam had no money. The officer drew his pistol. Looking Rostam straight in the eye, he said, 'Did you know I can kill you?'

What happened next defies belief. 'He took the safety catch off, aimed the pistol at me and fired, from a distance of one and a half metres. He was aiming at my forehead. At the last moment I moved my head a little and the bullet hit me in the mouth.' Pulling down his lower lip, Rostam showed me where the round had gone into his lower right jaw, smashed out a tooth,

236

travelled down his neck and lodged in his shoulder. Too dangerous to extract, it is still there. 'I could see my reflection in the mirror. There was blood everywhere. My friend picked me up and started shouting at the policeman. I croaked, "Call an ambulance for me." The policeman yelled back, "If you want an ambulance, go to the street and use a public phone."'

Contacting Gavahar, Rostam pressed charges. The case took more than a year to come to court. The policeman was found guilty and sentenced to nine years in jail, but such action takes real determination, persistence and courage on the part of the victim.

With the economy steaming ahead and the country's birth rate in free fall, the Russian government is keen to attract skilled immigrant labour to help keep the boom going. It is therefore just a bit ironic that neo-Nazi gangs like the NSO are training for 'war' against the very people on whom the state believes its future depends. And a minority of Moscow's police force seems to be lending a hand.

My final stab at getting under the National Socialist Union's skin was to accept an invitation to a day's 'country training' at what Dimitri Rumyansev proudly told me was the gang's secret rural headquarters. The location was so secret they took the batteries out of our mobile phones so no one could track them. Unfortunately, they also rammed stinking old woollen balaclavas with no eyeholes over our heads, including that of our translator Elena. The gangsters made us wear them all the way to our destination, which turned out to be two hours distant. Strangely, no one seemed to notice the absurdity of leaving Andy free to carry on filming while the rest of us were blindfold, but by now I had come to the conclusion that logic wasn't really the gang's strongest suit.

We were decanted into the grounds of a nondescript red-brick dacha located I will never know where. It was a good size, but hardly Hitler's Eagle's Nest. A set of steep steps led up to an imposing front door. Lined up on either side of this staircase was the rest of the NSO. In among the ragtag crew of about two dozen people, two individuals attracted my eye. The first was Tesak, a hulking young brute with a head-lice haircut and a constellation of scars – especially on his fists – he told me proudly were the result of knife wounds. 'Scars are decorations for a fist. It's beautiful to have a scar. They are combat wounds.'

'What kind of combat?' I asked.

Tesak pulled a massive knife from his belt and showed it to me. Its handle was embossed with a Russian bear. 'From fights with the blacks,' he said. 'In a fight you don't always notice immediately that your enemy has a weapon, you just feel the blood running from your arm – but what can you do? In the desert there are aggressive wild animals. You have to hunt them. If you don't, they attack the peaceful population ... If you kill one of them, then a thousand immigrants won't come.'

Tesak said he had become a racist after Chechens supposedly blew up several blocks of Moscow flats in 1999. 'In the first block of flats lived a girl I knew. I said, "Let's go and kill Chechens." I took a knife and saw some guys with clubs. They saw my mood and said, "Come with us." We went to a market and punished some Chechens for the crime committed by their compatriots.'

The dacha was immaculately clean and, as is usual in Russia, I had to remove my shoes before entering. No one would say who owned the place, but it was well furnished, well looked after and comfortable. Somewhere in the background lurked a wealthy politician or business sponsor willing to lend out his mansion for neo-Nazi use. The 'library' contained only five books, one of which was a Russian translation of Hitler's *Mein Kampf*. There were no flags flying outside and no other gang or racist symbols on display. When I commented on this, Rumyansev said they did not want to upset the neighbours.

After the world's longest tour – three interminable hours – it was time to go outside and see what the gang members were doing for their country training. What they were doing was cavorting about in the large gardens, learning basic unarmed combat moves as they had been when I met them in the Moscow gym, only this time in the open air. As usual, Rumyansev was standing on the sidelines, watching, and as it was a hot sunny day, the guys had stripped to their shorts. The whole scene looked like a very bad Russian remake of a Nazi-era propaganda film.

The other person who had stood out from the crowd when I saw them beside the steps was a slight, diminutive sixteen-year-old girl with dusty blonde hair. Katy described herself as the gang's Web content manager. She attended the American School in Moscow and spoke very good English with an American accent. Katy was a strange one: why was a nice-looking girl from a rich family hanging around with this lot? She sat me down at a laptop and showed me her 'Nazi artwork', which consisted of cartoon images of Hitler in his underwear done Walt Disney style. She also showed me Tesak's home videos of racist gang attacks on immigrants. To my eyes, a couple of these looked staged, but another video was a Ku Klux Klan propaganda film in which a man is first hung by the neck until dead and then hacked to pieces. Only too real, it was horrifying.

I couldn't help thinking that elsewhere in the world, in places like Rio de Janeiro and El Salvador, people join gangs in the generally mistaken belief that this will make them wealthy, earn them kudos or at least help them stay alive. The NSO, in contrast, are together out of straightforward racial hatred.

A voice shouted lunch was ready, and we went back outside to the garden. Someone had been pushing the neo-fascist boat out: trestle tables were groaning under the weight of a large buffet. Among the dishes on offer was a white mayonnaise and cream cheese pie decorated with a swastika carefully piped on top of it in bright red tomato ketchup. While we were eating – and since I like to eat with friends or at the very least people who are not racists it was hard to get the food down – young Katy came up to me and made a confession. 'Well, I killed one man.'

I stared at her. 'You killed a bloke?' She nodded and shot me a cheeky smile.

'How did you do that?'

'With a knife.' She smiled again. 'But I won't do it any more. I had to.'

'Why did you have to?'

'To make friends with all these people.' She indicated the rest of the gang. 'It was just to see how it feels. I don't like killing. It's not funny.'

Katy liked the camera; Katy wanted to be a star. I think Katy would, as a result, have said just about anything to shock me. I allowed myself the comfort of disbelieving her account of stabbing an immigrant to death. Especially when she went on to add, 'I think the robots will kill all the humanity – we'll all die.' Do you want to believe a sixteen-year-old girl goes around the Moscow transport system killing people because they look slightly different to her? Me neither.

Rumyansev sidled up to me in his crab-like way and drew me to one side. Pointing at the gang members munching their way through large helpings of swastika pie, he outlined his political agenda. 'These young men and women,' he told me, 'are tomorrow's Russian government. When we take power, we will clean all the weak, corrupt officials from government.' Watching Tesak the Incredible neo-Nazi Hulk wolfing down hunks of barbecued meat, I tried to imagine him as the Russian finance minister. Somehow, I couldn't quite get the vision to work for me.

I asked Rumyansev what he would say to those people who found the views and behaviour of the NSO shocking. He said, 'I would like the viewers in Europe to remember the bombs on the London Underground. What's happening in Holland. What happened in France, Holland and Madrid. If they don't like our philosophy after that, then those people don't deserve to be called people.'

Before we parted company, Katy dressed up for the cameras in full Ku Klux Klan rig, but the point of her conical hat kept flopping over to the side. It gave her a slightly comic air, rather like Dopey in Disney's *Snow White and the Seven Dwarfs*. She seemed fond of Disney. I asked Tesak how you kept the point of your Klan hat stiff. Did starch help, or was there some other way of keeping it up? I don't think Tesak quite saw the joke.

Back in Moscow we said goodbye to the NSO for the last time. Staying in character, Rumyansev once again gave the Sieg Heil! salute. I looked at the rest of the crew. 'Byeee!' we called out in best camp style, waving goodbye with limp wrists. Taking the micky was our way of letting off steam. Still, my time in

Moscow made me feel that for all their foibles we should take neo-Nazi gangs like the NSO seriously. Their numbers are swelling. And too many people thought Hitler was a joke in the 1930s.

As I turned to leave, Sasha came forward and gave me a box of scented candles. A farewell present. I am pretty sure they weren't laced with Semtex, but I left them behind anyway.

Beware neo-Nazis bearing gifts.

7. Jamaica

That first Friday evening we accepted an invitation from the Kingston murder squad to film a typical night shift. It was a balmy Jamaica night with a cooling breeze blowing down from the hills. The Undertaker's Breeze they call it locally. In the evening it takes over from the onshore Doctor Breeze that helps cool the intense daytime heat. The Undertaker rustled the tall coconut palms and the leaves of the sea almonds outside the hotel.

I didn't know it yet, but the undertaker was going to be busy.

We reached the central police station at around 8.00 p.m. Just crossing the road to get there was a near-death experience – the traffic in Jamaica doesn't hang about. And it doesn't stop. Settling in for a long night, I popped a boiled sweet in my mouth. Before I had finished it, the radio crackled into life. 'Man shot dead, Lincoln Road. Please attend immediately.' The location was close to Jubilee Market, where the witchy woman had put her mark on me a couple of days before.

Just before leaving the UK I had had a minor oper-ation to remove a mole from my back. It had only needed a few stitches, but the wound was not yet healed. Standing in the crowded Jubilee Market on our second day, sweltering in the downtown Kingston heat, all of a sudden I felt pain flare across my back. I spun round. A tiny, stick-skinny, wizened old woman was standing a yard away, grinning at me. The dark brown eyes were uncannily bright, as if she knew me and all my secrets. A policeman standing by the stall next to us murmured, 'You better watch out – she is a witchy woman.'

I stared at this complete stranger. Of all the places she could have pinched me . . . It was as if she had known it was there. And what was the evil grin about? With a last knowing look the woman turned and disappeared into the crowd. I asked Andy Thomson, our cameraman, to look at the damage. All the stitches had burst and the cut was wide open. For the rest of my time in the market the blood ran down my back and mixed with the sweat.

For a European, downtown Kingston is the other side of the street. If I had not known that before, I was sure of it now. The incident left me feeling unsettled, much as I felt now. It isn't every day you get invited to a murder.

We jumped in the cars and drove towards Lincoln Road at high speed, the police in their Suzuki four-by-fours, blue top lights flashing and our driver doing a great job to keep up with them. Kingston sits in a punchbowl: the rich live on the surrounding hills while the poor sweat it out on the flats. We were headed downtown, to the heartland of Kingston's gang turf.

Reaching the crime scene in less than ten minutes, we stepped out. There was an unmarked white police car sideways across the road and beyond that a line of blue and white tape guarded by armed uniformed officers. They asked us to wait our side of the fluttering plastic. Beyond it, in the darkness, I suddenly made out the body of a black male lying in the road with his eyes wide open. You never quite get used to seeing violent death. There was an officer kneeling beside the man. Two detectives in armoured vests, white surgical gloves and with powerful scene-of-crime lamps walked up and bent over the dead man, pulling and poking at his clothes like looters. A loud burst of laughter came from somewhere close at hand, and there was the steady background thump of a dance track. Dogs attracted by the smell of blood prowled in the hope of a feed. An officer in dark blue coveralls and black boots armed with an M16 moved very slowly around the man, then stopped and pointed the weapon at something he could see on the ground. The object gleamed yellow as the light caught it – a cartridge case. The remains of what looked like a takeaway meal of jerk chicken lay scattered off to one side. A uniformed policeman was positioning yellow numbered markers next to the shell cases and other objects of interest around the body. So far, he had reached number nine.

Once they had carried out their initial exmination,

the murder squad detectives invited us in through the line. The dead man's open eyes gleamed in the darkness. Walking towards him, I had the strangest sensation he was still alive, just lying there very still, staring at me. As the detectives trained their lamps on him the detail of his death jumped out with shocking clarity. Aged about forty, he was lying on his front with his face turned slightly to the left. He had been thickset and strong, with broad features. Both arms were folded partly under him, hands up beside his shoulders as if he had been about to perform a press-up. There was a trickle of blood from a wound to the left forearm. He had a high forehead with a tight scrub of greying hair receding from the temples. His body was riddled with bullets.

Shot repeatedly through the buttocks and back, a section of lung had been blown out through his mouth. Bright red, it projected like an extra tongue. The underside of the body and the hard-packed light brown earth around it was a lake of thick, dark red blood. A single shot had been fired into the man's head behind the right ear. A trail of blood led to the spot where he had finally fallen. Except perhaps for his age, there was nothing to mark him out as the victim of a suspected gang execution. He was not wearing any jewellery and his pockets had contained little cash. The dogs started barking and a fight broke out between two of them. A policeman shooed them away.

There is little dignity in death and there was none at

all for this man. Murder squad officers who do this kind of thing every day are not respectful when it comes to handling a corpse. A detective yanked down the dead man's dark grey jeans and patterned underpants and began measuring the size of the bullet holes in his exposed backside. A second officer pulled up the black T-shirt to measure the entry wounds peppering the torso and then stripped him of that, too. Rigor mortis had not yet set in and the corpse was still malleable. A yellow marker with the number 14 was positioned squarely in the small of the man's back. A pale dog made it in through the cordon and started licking at the blood. I waited until the senior investigating officer had counted the entry wounds. 'Eighteen shots. Somebody didn't like him.'

Fired at close range, they were mostly 9-millimetre rounds but the kill shot to the head was a .45 calibre bullet. A gang killing, almost certainly. A friend of the victim had been with him at the time of the attack and had somehow escaped with nothing more than a leg wound. He might be able to help the police identify the attackers.

A crowd was gathering. The onlookers included several small children who stared wide-eyed at the mess on the ground. But some of the adults were laughing and jeering at the dead man. As their numbers grew the police advised us to leave. Before we did so, the detective inspector in charge told me, 'So far, we've ascertained that at about 8.15 tonight a gentleman by the name of Roy Grant was shot and killed while he walked along the thoroughfare here. We have found seventeen spent shells. It could have been gang-related – a lot of shots have been fired. But Roy Grant was not known to us.' A van arrived. Two policemen got out, laid a stretcher on the ground next to the body, picked it up, put it on the stretcher, covered it with a white shroud and put the whole thing in the back of the vehicle. They left behind the dead man's shoes, which they had presumably forgotten. Those, and a broad pool of glistening blood. The DI added, 'The people in this area didn't like him, either.'

'How do you know that?' I asked.

'If they like someone who's been killed, they throw stones at us when we come to investigate the crime scene. And no one is talking about taking revenge, which is what they usually do when they liked the person who died. We think Mr Grant was from another area – he was just walking through the wrong part of town. What we have to watch out for now is someone in *this* area getting shot in revenge. They always do it straight away.'

Their work done, the detectives began peeling off their white plastic gloves. One of them said, 'This kind of shooting happens all the time.'

After six hours of filming we went back to the hotel, had a cold beer and ate our fill of jerk chicken. Maybe the casual attitude to death in Jamaica was catching.

*

I was in Jamaica to find out how one of the world's most beautiful countries came to have such a bad gang problem. I read up a bit to get an overview. It was quickly clear that nowhere else in the world is a country's gang problem so catastrophically bound up with its politics. There are two major political parties: the Jamaica Labour Party (JLP) and the People's National Party (PNP). In the late 1970s and in the run-up to the 1980 general election, politicians on both sides armed people in Kingston's garrisons, or local neighbourhoods, to bring in the vote – if necessary at gunpoint. The result was slaughter on the streets, as armed gangs from either side of the political divide fought for control of the garrisons. In the end the government that had taken power by implementing this organized insanity had to call in the army to stop it.

But the killing hasn't ever stopped. The gangs have simply shifted shape, and if anything grown even more murderous. In 2006 Jamaica achieved the dubious distinction of overtaking its closest rivals as the country with the highest number of homicides per head: 69 per 100,000, compared with 44 in South Africa and Colombia's 41. Since the vast majority of these murders take place in Kingston, this means that in a city roughly the size of Leeds four or five people are killed by violence every day.

As a way of rewarding the neighbourhoods that had voted for them, the politicians handed jobs and money out like sweeties to the 'dons' or garrison leaders. The dons distributed the work and the money – 'spoils' – to the people under their control and everyone was happy. Unless they lost out, in which case the usual thing was to pick up a gun and take someone else's spoils. One of the most coveted sources of income for a garrison community was 'gully work' – clearing rubbish and muck from the wide, deep storm drains, known as gullies, that take the run-off from the hills around Kingston and flush it to the sea. As much as three metres across and two metres deep, some of these gullies form borders between the garrisons. You know at once when you are in a gang-controlled area by the massive murals painted on the gully walls, often smiling portraits of the local don, and by the graffiti that proclaim the gang's control; the pictures, signs and symbols tell you which gang holds sway in that part of town.

Over the past few years, like Frankenstein's monster, Kingston's gangs have run out of control. From what I could make out, there are two main reasons for this: drugs and money, each inextricably entwined with the other. With the global increase in drug consumption, the garrison dons have been quick to see that if they can make money selling marijuana on the island, or better still cutting themselves a slice of Jamaica's massive cocaine transhipment pie, then, hey, who needs the politicians? And the drugs pie really is massive: every year roughly a tenth of all the cocaine on its way to the US from Latin America passes through Jamaica –

billions of dollars' worth – together with a fair tonnage of best-quality marijuana. The island is also popular with Colombian cartels looking to launder their ill-gotten gains.

The new drugs income has freed Jamaica's gangs from political control, allowing them to do their own thing. With great power has come great irresponsibility. Not content with dealing and shipping drugs, the gangs have turned to other crimes, especially extortion and assassination, to swell their coffers. Most of the island's gang warfare now comes down to claiming and holding turf, and beating off your nearest rivals at any cost. Who holds the ground makes the money – simple as that. The politics has got lost in the violence, and plain greed has risen to the top. As a result, the gangs are growing in number and splintering. The frontier lines between the garrison gangs are shifting ever faster, and the people who live in gang-controlled neighbourhoods suffer an ever-rising tide of violence and fear. As if the garrison gangs were not bad enough, sub-gangs have sprung up across Kingston, next-door in Spanish Town and now even in the tourist destination of Montego Bay – dozens of them, small groups of criminally minded armed youths who control a 'corner' or very small patch of turf, often as not just a single street.

Jamaica's corner gangs are the least organized and loosest of any I had seen and therefore very hard to pin down. A man might pick up a gun one day and put it down the next. He might be working in a legal job and as a gangster part time. Sometimes, he might hire himself out to the opposition or switch allegiance to a rival gang. This chaos makes the island's gangsters more, and not less, lethal. And harder for the police to control.

The Grants Pen garrison I went to visit next day has a very good example of the new type of gang that has taken over from the old-style political model. Unique in being a gang-run ghetto bang in the middle of a much more upmarket district, Grants Pen is currently divided between four warring factions, the largest and most dangerous being the High End and Low End crews. They are all affiliated to the PNP, but that doesn't stop them fighting. To help me get an insight into the situation Marta Shaw, our assistant producer, had fixed for me to talk to Fast Mover, the don or leader of High End. We were meeting him on neutral ground of his choosing. We couldn't go into Grants Pen because it was too dangerous. The police regularly visit the garrison in force, and only three days previously they had shot dead a member of Fast Mover's crew while he was listening to his iPod.

A local man named Donovan was one of our conduits to the gang.

'Is the current crop of gangsters worse than the ones you knew as a child?' I asked him.

'Absolutely. It's barbaric now.'

'Can anything be done to stop the violence?'

He looked doubtful. 'It's embedded in this "bad man" culture. Who's the baddest man? Who's the cruellest man? Who's the vilest?' He mimicked the singsong gang style of speech: ' "My shoot a man with three shots." "*My* shoot a man with *one* shot." Who gets the highest ranking? It's simplified right down to that – a rating. Irrespective that this is a human life we're talking about.'

We waited in a downtown location for our contact to arrive. A vehicle appeared and stopped in front of our hired jeep. The man inside gave us the look that said what it needed to say and we began following him to our unknown destination. As with other garrisons, Grants Pen stops drive-by shootings by blocking access roads with tyres, bedsteads, old cookers, bits of angle iron and any other scrap that serves the purpose. 'Bleachers' or gang lookouts watch on corners and from rooftops for signs of enemy gangs, or to give warning of a police raid. The gangs also set up 'telltales' – traps that give away strangers. Approaching a round-about our driver slowed, checked left and right and then started going round it the wrong way. Just like the car in front. 'Hang on,' I said. 'What are you doing? Are you trying to get us killed?'

He laughed. 'It's the other way around, my friend. If we circle the right way, the gang will start shooting. Everyone here knows that.'

Except me. We pulled up suddenly. I had no idea where we were, but what I did know was that the gangsters lined up in front of me were heavily armed. We met in a kind of cross passage in the middle of some derelict buildings. There was rubble everywhere, the homes had lost their roofs and weeds were taking hold of what remained. Fast Mover's personal body-guard had on grey jeans, a maroon sweat top with orange sleeves, a fake Burberry beanie pulled down low over his forehead and a light blue and white bandanna pulled up over his nose. He wore a wide gold-coloured belt with a big diamanté buckle in the shape of a skull and crossbones. Gangster chic. But the most prominent feature of his outfit for me was the big Ruger P80 9-millimetre pistol I could see sticking out of his pocket.

Fast Mover was short and wiry. In blue jeans and a white T-shirt he too wore a beanie and a bandanna covering the lower half of his face. Like his bodyguard, he had a heavy gold chain around his neck. They let me examine the Ruger. It was in good working con-dition and fully loaded. When I asked to see the rest of their arsenal, they produced a Glock semi-automatic pistol with twin front ejection ports to speed up its rate of fire. Skull and Crossbones stepped back around the corner of the building and then produced a tiny black and silver pistol from an unseen mate. Easy to conceal in a boot top. 'If the police came here now there'd be a lot of shooting,' Fast Mover said with a laugh.

Without warning, the previously unseen gang member stepped into view holding an AK-47 assault rifle. I said, 'That would get rid of any intruders.' The new man wore gaudy patterned shorts with a white cotton shirt pulled up over his head, leaving a narrow slit for the eyes. He had some trouble releasing the AK-47's magazine. Fast Mover took the weapon, detached the mag and handed it to me. Like the other firearms, it was fully loaded.

I said, 'Where do these weapons come from – Haiti?'

Now brandishing a Browning 9-millimetre pistol, Fast Mover sang out, 'It's a Haiti P80,' as if he were reciting a nursery rhyme.

Guns are pouring into the country from every direction in a drugs for weapons exchange between Jamaica's gangs, Colombian narcotics traffickers and Haitian gunrunners. A boat laden with compressed locally grown ganja and/or hash oil puts to sea and meets a vessel from Haiti – or sometimes Honduras – with a cargo of guns: AK-47s, M16s and Bushmaster AR-15 assault rifles, Glocks, Browning M9s and Ruger P80 pistols. The guns come into Jamaica, the dope goes to Haiti or Honduras and on to the USA and everybody's happy – or at least they are if they are in the loop. The cocaine travels by all kinds of routes, not least the 'go-fast' speedboats that roar between Jamaica and its neighbours nightly.

We moved into one of the ruined rooms and sat down on some white plastic garden chairs. Softly spoken and highly articulate, Fast Mover told me that as the don of High End he tried to help the poor people in the area by giving them money. 'I give their parents lunch money for some of their children. Things like that.' A regular Robin Hood, just like the old-style political dons. He said that things were better now in the community in that more money filtered down from the government, but, 'Still you have people living in great poverty.' When I asked how he had become the don he said, 'It just came natural. By defending people, I got their applause. I share a lot of thoughts with them, and positiveness. The people have to choose you. I didn't choose this life. This life chose me.'

'What would you say to any young person who was thinking of joining a gang?'

'I would say sometimes it's not what they choose. Sometimes it chooses them, because of the environment where they are living.'

'What about some of the young men in the world who think joining a gang is glamorous?'

'I don't know about people who think it's a great life. I'm really fighting for a cause. I can't go and do a nine-to-five job. I'll live this life until I die. It's not like I can leave it.'

'What about your children? What if they wanted to take up this kind of life?'

He shook his head. 'I wouldn't want them to take up this kind of life. I would like the best for them. Have a nice job and take care of their father!' He told me he used to drive a taxi before joining the gang. Aged twenty-four, he was philosophical about his chances of making it to his next birthday: 'I get rich or die trying.

I got no worries about dying. Death is part of what I do – either me causing it, or me dying.' He ticked off his objectives in life on his fingers: 'Gold, women, respect.' A gang leader for no more than a couple of years, Fast Mover claimed to own five or six houses, three or four cars and have 'some very nice girls' at his beck and call.

'Why do you think some women find gangsters attractive?'

'Maybe they just like the glamour and the fame. But there's a price to pay. They think it's like a movie star kind of thing. But this is not a movie. People get killed.'

'Some people told me there was a direct connection between you, the area don, and the MP of the PNP. Does that still happen?'

'That's the old style. I don't need the MP.'

'Does he have contacts with other gangs in the community?'

'He does have contacts with other gangs. Before, the politicians used to give the gangs guns. But it's not like that any more. Gangs get their own guns. The politicians still play a part, but it's not a major part like it was.'

'Does the fact that this is an election year mean that you will have extra problems?' Fast Mover nodded. 'Yes. Because I will have to pick a side.'

'So if you pick JLP or PNP, there will be a problem from the other side. How will that show itself?'

'Guys will come in hard with guns. And the police –

whatever side they choose, they will come. I seen some dark stuff. A man in my position, the next thing the police will shoot him. But I want to say this: if you have a gun, there is a consequence to pay. So if you are not prepared, I don't think you should ever touch it.'

'Why do you think parts of Jamaica are so violent?'

'Sometimes I think that the people who make the movies – that has a lot to do with people taking up this kind of life. Because everybody wants to be a movie star.' He laughed. 'Tourists go to the north coast or the hills; they don't see the hard man community.'

'What could be done to change things for the better?'

'Well, I'd like to see the government come in and put in some ways and means so the kids can have a better schooling. Right now the children have to pay when they go to high school. For education I don't think you should pay so much.'

'What do you think the future holds for you?'

'The future depends on if I live or die. If I live, I see a bright future. I can take my time and get to the top. Not if I go to prison. From my point of view, the majority of people in Jamaica are gangsters. I think the police are gangsters. I think the prime minister is a gangster. But they are high-level gangsters.'

Either free to cross gang boundaries at will or insanely rash, Fast Mover later arrived at my hotel behind the wheel of a top-end saloon car, or 'low rider' as they are known in Jamaica. Favoured marques are Mercedes, BMW and the Lexus saloon Fast Mover was driving. Over a cold beer, Fast Mover said that as well as defending their local turf he and his two dozen crew made money by extortion, drug dealing and contract killings. Shopkeepers routinely pay the gangs $500 a month or more protection money.

Many assassinations are requested by business people seeking to eliminate the competition. A car dealer, for example, might come to Fast Mover and say, 'I've got a problem with Mr X – his garage is taking a lot of my business. How much to take care of the problem?' The answer, Fast Mover told me, varied according to the difficulty of the job. But for a man's life it was ludicrously low – hundreds not thousands of Jamaican dollars. He was frank about his methods of killing: 'You have to find a man's weakness. Everyone got a weakness – drugs, women, drink. We got girls in the gang we can use, or we pay a girl. She lure a man to his death just like that.' He snapped a couple of lean fingers.

However such killings are done, they are disastrous for the island's legitimate businesses. Every year they pay roughly 7 per cent of their profits to the gangs in protection and 75 per cent of Jamaica's college graduates leave to seek work abroad. Every year more and more businesses move with them, helping the cycle of poverty and joblessness that fuels the gangs. And the violence.

In the three days we were filming in Grants Pen two people died – the police shot dead a High End member and a High End gunman murdered a Low End rival –

and a family was burned out of its home. Fast Mover told me he hated the Low End crew 'because they have spilled blood. Our blood. And we will take them out.'

This was exactly the same kind of tit-for-tat killing I'd seen elsewhere in the world: small gangs, living and operating in areas separated by a street or a wall, locked in a spiral of mutual killing. And, as elsewhere, the irony was that the rival gangsters lived in the same kind of homes, had the same interests, wore similar clothes, listened to the same music, ate the same food and drove the same kind of cars.

In Jamaica, more often than not, their fathers and grandfathers had been involved in the island's earlier political killing, and it was a matter of family honour to keep fighting. I asked Fast Mover, 'Is there any end to this?'

He shook his head. 'No.'

I left Fast Mover with his bodyguard – the pair of them looking over their shoulders for the rest of their lives.

The following Monday I went to see Caroline Gomes, who has been running the civil rights and pressure group Jamaicans for Justice since the 1999 Kingston riots, when there was widespread shooting, looting and burning, a countrywide police and army lockdown and many people died. Gomes said the aims of the group were to help the public get justice from the police and the government, and to document cases of official abuse as a way of advocating change. 'People die here very anonymously,' she said, 'and are labelled criminals because they die at the hands of the police. People want society to know that their sons or daughters were not criminals . . . We are trying to get the government to do something about police killings.'

'How many of those killings get to court?'

'Very few. We find that when we do actually get a verdict of criminal responsibility on the part of the police we run into a blockade at the state level. In the last ten years we have had one policeman convicted.'

'How many killings by the police last year?'

'Two hundred and twenty-six. The last ten years we've had close to 1,600 deaths at the hands of the police. As the police concentrate on the area of Kingston, the criminals grab a car and travel. We've had some awful cases outside Kingston – situations where the police have drawn their guns and fired because a crowd are angry. The police are supposed to carry a gun in self-defence and use proportionate force. But . . .'

'Some people have told us the police act as judge, jury and executioner.'

'If it's what the police call a "righteous shooting" – people shooting at them, bad gang action – then people don't come to us. But we get about 30 per cent of cases where people feel deeply that an execution occurred or there was a serious breach of police procedure. I don't know how much of the horror stories you want, but there was a killing where seven young men died. They were locked up in a concrete building with metal windows. The police story is that they came to execute a warrant, they were fired on and returned fire. Seven people were found dead; not one policeman received a scratch. The story from the residents was that they took a "Judas coat" [an informer or traitor] with them. He got the men inside to open the door and the police went in and executed them. Amnesty International investigated it extensively. Expert testimony said they were killed point blank. Six of the seven had multiple gunshot wounds in their head. The youngest was fifteen.

'Jamaica has a two-sided image. It's the sun, sea, sand beautiful tourist destination: Bob Marley, "One Love", Rastafari. And then the other half is a horribly violent place where "The police have to do what they have to do." So we have had a hard time drawing it not only to international but to local attention. The tactic of killing people to solve a case actually breeds murder, and it is ineffective. It's something we've been doing now in Jamaica for forty years. It hasn't controlled our murder rate: we have a rising murder rate. The British government has put a lot of money into police reform. While I accept that is important, my problem has been the lack of accountability.'

I asked Gomes about links between the island's politicians and the gangs.

'It started with the politicians and now they have lost control. But the links remain. Those gangs have nominal ties, and sometimes beyond nominal ties, to the political parties. So you have well-known dons who are big social figures who no longer live in the community. And they'll have birthday parties where politicians turn up. They'll have funerals at which ministers of government turn up. The very strong political ties allow [the politicians] to get out the vote at election time. We feel strongly that's why we can't get a handle on it – because the links are too deep and too long-standing. I'm not sure we have much justice.

'The police can only operate as they operate because the leadership above them allows it. If we change the leadership and ask them to be accountable, then the police will change. It can occur. We've seen communities like August Town and Fletcher's Land taking charge of themselves. We've got to build and keep pointing out the hypocrisy . . . Only mad people keep doing what they've been doing over and over again and expecting different results. We've got to try a different way. You've got to be an eternal optimist to do this work: believe it can happen and it will happen and it must happen. The choices are not nice otherwise.'

You have to hope there are more people out there like Caroline Gomes.

We went into Craig Town at noon, when it was boiling hot. Our guide, Wani, was a short, slim-built twenty-one-year-old with cornrows woven tight to his head. He wore a white singlet and kept a cigarette tucked permanently behind his ear. He and the rest of his dozen or so crew occupied a 200-metre-square Craig Town block bordering Benbow, the neighbouring and enemy downtown garrison. Even in the blazing sunlight it felt really, really dangerous. Not because anyone was sticking a gun in my face, but because the Craig Town gang were convinced the Benbow crew next door would be jealous of our presence. Craig Town, Trench Town, Arnett Gardens and Jones Town were all once part of the same PNP community, but when the police killed the overall don in 2004 the area descended into a lethal power struggle that is still being fought. As far as Wani and his mates were concerned, they were not actually a criminal gang: they only did what was necessary to defend their turf from other crews.

Wani took me on a tour of their turf. We walked down a narrow street intersecting with more of the same at right angles. The single-storey one-bedroom houses were painted in once bright but now faded colours, and all of their roofs were corrugated iron. Once decent family homes, they had long since deteriorated to shanties, not improved by the bullet strikes that had chewed lumps out of the walls, or in the case of high-velocity rounds, drilled right through them. Many were now home to more than one family, crammed together into a couple of rooms in the sweltering heat. We came on a stretch of houses that had been gutted, only the broken walls standing as if they had been bombed. 'The people ran away,' Wani told me.

'Why did they run away?'

He pointed at a broken section of boundary wall. 'They came through there. They were shooting everywhere.' He made a noise like a kid playing war – '*Brrrrrp!*' 'They' were the opposition Benbow gangsters, the kind who had been eyeballing us from the other side of the invisible dividing line down the street. A little bit further on there was a shop selling dry goods. Bullets had shattered its plate-glass frontage in several places. A lot of the holes were at head height.

Ray, one of Wani's mates said, 'AK. AK-47.'

We reached the corner and turned into a main road. It led us along to a primary school with walls painted light blue. 'There was a shoot-up in here,' Wani told me.

In the school? We turned in at the gate. A sign above the main entrance read, 'St Simon's Basic School & Community Centre'. In dozens and dozens of places the light blue plaster of the playground walls had been filled and overpainted in a darker blue to cover the bullet holes. I counted 300 during a break in filming and then gave up. Wani said, 'They jumped over that wall.' He pointed at the high wall on the playground's far side. 'Over there is Benbow. That's where they come from.' Inside the school I could hear an infant class reciting a lesson. It was lucky the shooters had come at night.

When we came back out, Wani's friend pointed up the street. 'There was a man ran a Shell station up there. He kept a gun to defend himself. A crew came and shot him for his guns. They knew he had them under the counter.' He made a looping gesture with his hands around his neck. 'Then they took his gold chains. So now we got no more petrol here.'

Wani led on. We squeezed along an alley almost too tight to turn in walled with corrugated iron. 'Back of the yards,' he said, pointing at the patched, rusting sheets to either side. Occasionally there were open spaces with piles of junk. 'We safe here,' Wani assured me. 'The dangerous place is the boundary between gangs.' I hoped he was right.

In the middle of Craig Town we came across Charlie's Rum Bar. The breeze-block dive is run by the eponymous Charlie, a big laid-back fifty-year-old with a mass of long greying dreadlocks, a woollen hat in the Rastafarian colours, bright blue wraparound sunglasses and an interesting personal history. Charlie was very chilled. In fact he was almost monosyllabic. We sat down outside the bar. 'Why is it so violent here?' I asked him.

He gazed at me for a while and then uttered a single word: 'Hungry.'

The man sitting next to him nodded. 'People are fighting to live.'

Talking to Charlie and the others, I had an over-whelming sense of a community completely cut off: isolated in its hatred for anyone and everyone outside it and hated by them in return. Children are brought up to hate their neighbours just across the street, and blood is continually spilt between adjoining communities. The feeling of oppression, of hopelessness in the face of gang warfare, was tremendous. People gain identity from these tight-knit ghettos, but at the same time they lose any chance of a peaceful life.

Night came. The gang had promised to show me their arsenal of firearms. It was pitch dark. We were standing on a corner waiting for the gangsters when out of the night came the sound of a boy singing, one of the sweetest sounds I ever heard, a soaring solo hymn, something about 'Jesus will save you.' Glancing up at the five masked gangsters who had appeared around the corner on the other side of the road, I said, 'Let's hope He is not having a night off.' Sometimes a bit of silliness breaks the tension.

We went across. The leader said, 'We have our weapons, we are going on patrol. You can come with us.'

Right away, I felt something was wrong. The gangsters would not step forward out of the shadows to let me see them, even into the meagre light that came from the nearby church. They seemed to be holding weapons – pistols of some kind – but again something didn't look right. You handle a real gun in a certain way, not as they were doing, in a posing kind of style like something out of a bad television show. I said, 'Can we see your guns? Can you come forward into the light?'

One of the masks mumbled, 'No, man, we are not showing you,' and they turned and ran away.

We went after them. Our cameraman Andy kept

good pace, despite the weight of the equipment he had to lug. We've been stitched up, I thought. Those aren't real weapons. Worse, we were now in no-man's-land between the garrisons, a rubbish-strewn area of waste ground with dogs barking at us, the kind of place where you are asking to get shot.

The gang stopped and we caught up with them. In the faint light I could see that the mask who had spoken to me was holding a contraption made of scrap wood and a wire coat hanger made to look like a sub-machine gun. Brandishing this, he made '*pow*, *pow*' noises, the kind little boys make when they are playing at war or cops and robbers.

I stared at him. 'Why are you making those noises?' I asked. He turned ran off into the darkness again.

I turned to Andy and the rest of the crew. 'This is pointless. Let's stop filming, they're wasting everybody's time.' They'd promised to show us how they protected their community but when it came to it they wouldn't do it.

We'd been meant to stay on their turf overnight but now I said, 'Let's get out of here.' I told Colin, our fixer, and Sarah Manley, who had both done a great job helping us out, that we'd been duped. Back at Charlie's Rum Bar, which suddenly felt like a home from home, we had just sat down to have a beer when I noticed a small group of men staring at us. I recognized them by their clothing as the same masked crew who had just been giving us the runaround.

I stood up to go to the toilet. As I was passing the group, one of them leaned towards me and said, 'You want to see my ting?' Thankfully, he meant his gun.

'It's all right,' I said. 'It's too late now.'

His hand went to his waist and he drew out a small .22 pistol, the kind of Saturday night special a lady might once have carried in her handbag. As tings go, it really wasn't all that impressive.

'We were expecting more than that, mate,' I told him. A part of me was still angry. I told Charlie we had been let down. In a while he stood, moved slowly across to the group, had a quiet word with them and then came back.

'Be in the same place, ten o'clock tomorrow morning, and you will see what you want to see.' They escorted us back out to our vehicles. When we got there the next day, the gang were waiting – masked again, only this time in broad daylight. And with a police checkpoint right around the corner. They led us through a series of narrow, tin-walled rat runs and then stopped. They had definitely made an effort: there were two AK-47s, a pump action shotgun, several Glock pistols and an assortment of other 9-millimetre automatics. Enough to cause a lot of hurt.

There is no functioning social welfare system in Jamaica. The poor have to do what they can to survive – another major reason for the existence of the gangs. With the exception of the police, the emergency services frequently refuse to enter the most dangerous of the gang-held areas, for the simple reason that if they do go in to help, they are often fired on. What this means in practice is that if someone in, say, Craig Town gets shot and needs emergency medical treatment, his friends and family stick him in a wheelbarrow and push him to the nearest hospital. If he is lucky, the victim survives the ride. Lots don't make it, or if they do they lose a leg or an arm.

To help combat the gangs, the Jamaican authorities have brought in London Metropolitan Police detective Mark Shields. In Jamaica on secondment from the Met and now one of Jamaica's deputy police commissioners, Shields's task is formidable: to get the gangs out of the garrisons and to oversee a clean-up of the island's police force.

I met the imposing six-foot-six-inch Shields in Kingston's Jubilee Market. I am five foot eleven but I had to stand on a ledge so we could talk on camera without me looking silly. A non-stop riot of bustling crowds, violent colours, shouts and thumping reggae music under the blazing heat, Jubilee Market crowds in and around the hollow shells of some elegant crumbling colonial buildings on the edge of a park. I saw people picking up discarded chicken bones and rooting through dustbins for food. Strictly for the locals, the market is not on the list of recommended tourist destinations. Corralled behind the walls of their patrolled compounds, 99 per cent of the island's tourists never learn that it has a serious gang problem.

For Shields there was an ecstatic welcome. Many people think he might be the saviour they have been seeking – an outsider with no previous connections in the Jamaican police. If you think I might be overdoing it a bit by using the word 'saviour', you won't if I tell you that people were coming up and kissing his hand. Wandering around the market talking to shoppers before and after I met Shields, I found out why: most of them long to see Jamaica free of the gangs. They are sick of the whole politician–don connection, the corner gangs, the shootings, the drug-dealing and the death.

In 2004, Shields and Assistant Commissioner Glenmore Anthony Hinds launched Operation Kingfish, a high-profile anti-gang initiative aimed at toppling the top twelve dons and their crime syndicates and getting them and their violent foot soldiers out of the island's communities for good. To date, Kingfish has dismantled two gangs, the Giddeon Warriors and Lewis, and seriously disrupted a further seven: Dunkirk, Jack's Lane, Klansman, the One Ten Gang and the Top Road Gang, One Order and Mathews Lane. Its officers have either killed or arrested several dons; seized more than 1,800 firearms, large quantities of ammunition, more than fifteen tonnes of cocaine and some 2,000 kilos of compressed marijuana; and picked up more than 300 other people for a range of offences including murder, drug trafficking and possession of a firearm.

If Shields and Hinds don't succeed it won't be for lack of trying: all around the market and for that matter all around the island there are posters: 'Ring this freephone 811 number and help the police arrest a gangster in your community.' Is Kingfish working? Only time will tell. The police have received more than 1,000 calls in response to their plea for information. Many have resulted in arrests. Given past levels of public apathy, this is encouraging.

The island certainly needs someone with focus, power and will: the homicide map Superintendent Arthur Brown showed me in Denham Town police station in March 2007 is spattered with orange dots marking killings. 'These are not individual murders,' he told me. 'Each dot represents a cluster of murders – many, many murders. If we put a dot for every murder, you wouldn't be able to see the map for orange.'

'How many murders have there been since Christmas?' I asked.

He looked at me. 'More than one hundred – about four a day.' The map also had a great many red dots straggling across the board. I noticed they were in roughly straight lines. 'Those red dots are where my men have been involved in firefights with the gangs. As you can see, they more or less mark the frontiers between the gangs. Our officers get called in to stop a shooting, and then they become part of it.'

Many Jamaican police officers were open about the problem of corruption in the Jamaican police. This is not to say that every copper in Kingston is bent – far from it. But as long as a minority of them take bribes, things won't get straight on the streets.

Whether or not as a result of the island's criminal gangs, since the 1950s hundreds of thousands of Jamaicans have emigrated. And with some of them has gone the island's gang culture, implanted into Toronto, Miami, London – wherever the expat gangsters have set up shop. Some of these offshore gangsters keep in contact with their counterparts back home, mostly through dealing drugs. Scotland Yard estimates that impoverished young female Jamaican drug mules attempt to smuggle an average of 100 kilos of cocaine into the UK every week, almost always by swallowing the drug in sealed condoms and hoping to get past HM Customs and the X-ray machines. This has become so commonplace the UK has recently introduced a visa system for Jamaicans wishing to enter Britain.

The close connections between gangsters abroad and back home means a conflict that started out in Jamaica can get settled by means of a phone call to Toronto or London. 'You killed my brother in Craig Town. I'm going to have your brother killed to even things up. We know where he lives.'

One of the last people I met was another Craig Town resident. Carlton told me how his girlfriend and 'baby-mother' Jonelle King had been shot dead on the way to get some food. It happened just after Christmas last year. She was four months pregnant with their first child, but that didn't stop an unknown gunman stepping out of the shadows and killing Jonelle and her unborn baby.

Sitting on the bed in his room, Carlton told me how he felt when they told him the news. 'Horrified. Terrible. My mother and my sister talked to me and they helped me understand certain things. But we are all suffering.' In his khaki shorts and striped polo top, Carlton looked much younger than his nineteen years. He said he did not know who had shot his girlfriend. He showed me the photograph of Jonelle on the front cover of the funeral service programme he kept. She was beautiful. A lovely smiling girl in a white dress and matching broad-brimmed hat, Jonelle King had been seventeen years old when she died.

No one had been arrested for the murder. Carlton sat on the edge of his bed and slowly turned the pages of his dead girlfriend's funeral service. A polite and well-mannered young man, he told me if he ever managed to identify the gunman, he would kill him.

On my last day in Jamaica I was lucky enough to take a trip up into the Blue Mountains. There is nowhere more beautiful. There was a strong smell of wild ginger and eucalyptus, and the mountains in the distance really did look smoke blue. Staring at all of this beauty, it was impossible not to reflect on some of the horrors I had seen in the gang-controlled areas. Several things need to change before Jamaica turns into the kind of place where its people can live without fear. First, there has to be some serious investment in terms of education, jobs and housing in the most deprived areas; second, the minority of corrupt politicians has to be removed from office and replaced with honest people; and last, they have to break the gangs.

Easier said than done. If you grow up believing thieving is OK, if you grow up thinking it is normal to pick up a gun and shoot a guy in the next street, torch a home and burn out a family, that is what you will do. This is not to say bad environments always produce bad people. Plenty of Jamaicans born in the ghettos have had the courage and the will to make it up and out. But the island's political corruption, its insidious gang and gun culture, its role in the international drugs trade and the widespread poverty make it difficult to see how change can happen. Still, if you treat people decently then they usually behave decently. Sometimes it is that simple.

Most Jamaicans would rather sit and have a beer with you and chew the fat than take a bullet. Just like anyone else.

Conclusion

In the early months of 2007, London saw five young teenagers shot dead. Kids as young as ten are now reportedly carrying sub-machine guns in the capital. For many people gang culture is about murder. It's about rape, robbery, drugs, violence, death and hate. But a lot of other people – particularly young men under the age of twenty – have a completely different idea of what gangs are all about. Dazzled by the 'gangsta porn' they see rap artists, actors and musicians project on the TV and in films, they think gangs are about fast cars and even faster women, bling, champagne and the luxury condo in Bel-Air. Some global brands promote and manipulate gang culture: sports stores in some countries even separate their goods into gang colours, reinforcing the gang's own branding.

I was optimistic setting out on my journey to meet the gangs, and I'd be the first to admit that in all kinds of ways I have been lucky – lucky with the crews I've had around me; lucky with the access I've been able to gain through the kindness of strangers. What has surprised me is how many gangsters out there have been prepared to talk. I have been even more surprised to connect with a few. More than once I have been moved to tears.

Then there are the stories of how so many of the gangs got started in the first place: El Salvador's gangs born as a direct result of the country's vicious civil war; the South African Number gangs dreamed up by an early-twentieth-century Zulu bandit; New Zealand's Mongrel Mob formed by teenagers abused in the country's children's homes. You couldn't make this up – as is so often the case, reality is better than fiction.

Is *Gangs* doing any good? Hard to say for sure, but people now stop me less because of characters I've played on TV, and more because I present a programme about gangs and they are interested. Especially young people. Some of them want to see if I am going to stop a bullet, but most simply want to understand more of what's going on in the world.

Some people have accused me of glorifying gangsters. Nothing could be further from the truth. What we see in the series is men who have murdered their own sisters, men who've been raped in prison, victims who have been beaten, stabbed and shot to death, girls beaten and forced into street gangs and then branded with tattoos. I've met men with their faces melted away by crystal meth, a man whose six-month-old child killed himself with his father's gun and a sixteen-year-old neo-Nazi Moscow girl who wants to wipe 'blacks' from the face of the earth.

What have I learned in the course of making the series? The wider the gap between rich and poor, and the more poverty it has, the worse a country's gang problem will be. Gangs spring up when social structures are destroyed by sudden and drastic change: the civil war in El Salvador, the end of apartheid in South Africa, the collapse of communism in Russia. Some people join gangs because of peer pressure or to get the friendship, loyalty and respect they cannot find anywhere else. Some join because their attitude is, 'If I can't get it legally, I'm going to take it.' A gang gives many people a family, a purpose and a sense of identity. A lot of men told me they join gangs to get women.

What else? Give people a legitimate way out of poverty, give them equality, a way to succeed and gangs will stop flourishing. Of course however bad their circumstances, gangsters still make a choice. As one female ex-gang member told me, 'We may have all these things against us, but we are the ones who pull the triggers.' I've learned food in your stomach matters. And education and housing.

And I've learned how much home matters. In fact, when I came back from one recent gang trip, I knelt down and kissed the tarmac.

Acknowledgements

Thanks to Will Pearson, without whose talent this book would never have happened, and to my agent, Michael Foster.

Thanks to everyone who contributed to *Ross Kemp on Gangs*, the programme. I am indebted to the bravery and dedication of the researchers, directors and crews. In particular I'd like to thank Jackie Lawrence, Jarrod Gilbert, Andrew O'Connell from Sky and Clive Tulloh from Tiger Aspect.

I'd also like to thank everyone at Penguin, especially my editor Katy Follain.

I particularly want to thank all the people who risked their personal safety to talk to me.

He just wanted a decent book to read ...

Not too much to ask, is it? It was in 1935 when Allen Lane, Managing Director of Bodley Head Publishers, stood on a platform at Exeter railway station looking for something good to read on his journey back to London. His choice was limited to popular magazines and poor-quality paperbacks – the same choice faced every day by the vast majority of readers, few of whom could afford hardbacks. Lane's disappointment and subsequent anger at the range of books generally available led him to found a company – and change the world.

'We believed in the existence in this country of a vast reading public for intelligent books at a low price, and staked everything on it'
Sir Allen Lane, 1902–1970, founder of Penguin Books

The quality paperback had arrived – and not just in bookshops. Lane was adamant that his Penguins should appear in chain stores and tobacconists, and should cost no more than a packet of cigarettes.

Reading habits (and cigarette prices) have changed since 1935, but Penguin still believes in publishing the best books for everybody to enjoy. We still believe that good design costs no more than bad design, and we still believe that quality books published passionately and responsibly make the world a better place.

So wherever you see the little bird – whether it's on a piece of prize-winning literary fiction or a celebrity autobiography, political tour de force or historical masterpiece, a serial-killer thriller, reference book, world classic or a piece of pure escapism – you can bet that it represents the very best that the genre has to offer.

Whatever you like to read – trust Penguin.